POWER AND PORTFOLIOS

Best Practices for High School Classrooms

JIM MAHONEY

Foreword by James Strickland

HEINEMANN • Portsmouth, NH

Heinemann
A division of Reed Elsevier Inc.
361 Hanover Street
Portsmouth, NH 03801–3912
www.heinemann.com

Offices and agents throughout the world

Library of Congress Cataloging-in-Publication Data
Mahoney, Jim.
    Power and portfolios : best practices for high school classrooms / Jim Mahoney ; foreword by James Strickland.
        p.   cm.
    Includes bibliographical references (p. 171) and index.
    ISBN 0-86709-529-6 (alk. paper)
    1. Portfolios in education.   2. Language arts (Secondary).   I. Title.
LB1029.P67 M33 2002
428'.0071'2—dc21   2001006288

Editor: James Strickland
Production service: Melissa L. Inglis
Production coordination: Vicki Kasabian
Typesetter: PD&PS
Cover design: Joni Doherty
Manufacturing: Steve Bernier

Printed in the United States of America on acid-free paper
06 05 04 03 02 RRD 1 2 3 4 5

CONTENTS

FOREWORD

I remember meeting Jim Mahoney at least ten years ago; both of us were taking one of those airport shuttle buses to the NCTE (National Council of Teachers of English) conference hotel. We were both a little dazed from the plane ride but eager to see everyone at the conference. We were exchanging pleasantries across the aisle when Jim mentioned that he had enjoyed the latest issue of the *English Leadership Quarterly,* the NCTE journal that I edited at the time. I was surprised in the way that editors of small-circulation periodicals are surprised when they meet an actual reader. But Jim was no ordinary reader. For the rest of the bus ride, Jim shared what he thought of each article in detail and what he planned to incorporate into his lessons. Jim Mahoney's became the "face" I later gave to the journal's previously anonymous reader, the reader I considered when deciding if an article I was going to include had the right balance of informed theory and practical application. I often asked Jim to write something for the quarterly, and he always promised to think about it. But he never sent anything. He never considered what he did to be noteworthy or new enough for publication. Jim is just that modest. I was never able to convince him to write something for me until now. When I mailed an early draft of this manuscript to the editorial board, the response was predictable, at least to me. One editor told me, "when I read the manuscript, I was riveted! His style is accessible and entertaining, and I could not put it down!"

Jim Mahoney is indeed a modest man, a teacher who always credits his successes to the work of others. He always shares the laurels with his teaching colleague Jerry Matovcik, and with his friends Bill Picchioni, Richie Weismann, Frank Gallo, and Joe Quattrini. He feels guilty about using the ideas of Donald Graves and Nancie Atwell and repeatedly says that he is standing on the shoulders of giants. I cannot help but believe that these two scholars, in particular, would be thrilled to know how successfully Jim has used what they originally wrote for elementary and middle school students and adapted it for senior high students. Jim has even used his adaptations of their strategies with first-year students at the local community college. So, regardless of what this modest man tells you, the day-to-day practices he describes in this book are 100 percent Jim Mahoney.

Many teachers have tried to implement writing/reading workshop in their classes. Some have struggled to add it to their already crowded curriculum; some have tried it for a short time and abandoned it. Many of those who tried to replicate the successes of *In the Middle* became frustrated when it didn't seem to work the same magic with their student populations as it had with Atwell's students in Maine. But Jim Mahoney presents what someone called "the regular guy" approach to the workshop methodology. He's used it in middle school and high schools, from remedial to regular to honors classes. His experiences are certain to offer a convincing introduction to anyone who's new to the workshop concept, and to extend a renewed overture to teachers who have been reluctant to try workshops again.

It is almost commonplace today to say that writing should have a purpose and audience beyond the teacher, and most would agree that the portfolio offers a perfect means to give it that purpose and audience. In this book, Jim Mahoney explains the theory and the nitty-gritty details of putting together a portfolio in a way that's beyond a mere recipe for success. His students, who are active all year in writing/reading workshop, generate quarterly portfolios for evaluation and anticipate the creation of their final portfolios. They are so anxious that they're jazzed about it from the first week of class—word travels quickly in high school halls. They remain so absorbed by their final portfolios that they stay after the last day of classes to put on finishing touches. And when Jim asks his students to write, he writes alongside them; sometimes he writes in front of them, using a transparency, letting them see the tentative moves, corrections, and adjustments a writer makes.

Jim Mahoney is the sort of teacher they should make movies about, but the funny thing is that he wouldn't be the star—his students would be. At the end of a school day, it's typical to see Jim walking down the corridor with a satchel of student papers—literary letters, essays, stories, poems—a little reading to enjoy after dinner. On his summer vacations, Jim takes student portfolios with him, collections that he has asked to keep between school years so that he can savor them at his leisure. And his students are just as obsessive, wanting to know what he thinks of their latest effort and wondering what his take is on a variety of things. If I were to make a movie of Jim Mahoney's teaching career, it would have to be a sort of classroom version of *It's a Wonderful Life,* because Jim truly has no idea how many lives he's touched.

One of my favorite stories about Jim involves a workshop that he was giving for local teachers. The workshop was drawing to a close; teachers were packing up to go, when a woman in the back of the room began testifying in a loud voice. "Everything this man says is true," she vouched. She went on to tell this group of teachers how amazed she and her husband were about the transformation that had come over her son, a generally bright boy who never cared much for reading. Lo and behold, they came home one night and there was no television on, no stereo playing, no sight of the boy at all until they opened the door of his bedroom. There he was, lying on the bed, his nose buried in a novel. "Let me tell you, it works!" she concluded. Jim, of course, simply thanked her and praised the work that her son and his best friend had done in class.

In this book, Jim must share the work of fifty or more students with you; as editor, I trimmed the stories and work of at least another hundred, if only to keep the size of the chapters manageable. I've been in professional workshops that Jim's offered and I've been fortunate enough to see the student portfolios that he brings to conferences. They are everything he says and more.

When we borrow the metaphor of *coach* for writing teachers, Jim's the guy we're thinking of. As a former basketball, football, baseball, and soccer coach, he knows what it means to be demanding and supportive at the same time. But he's more of an inspirational Neoplatonic coach who fills his young writers with notions about the perfect line or phrase. He tells them of his secret passion for shooting hoops, not in a pickup game but alone by himself late in the evening—shooting baskets for hours on end, staring up at the hoop, listening to the clang of the rim as the ball hits it and the sound of the net snapping. It's repetitive and absorbing, like a Zen exercise. Jim says that "one good shot forces you to stay around and take more, just to feel that shot again." As their writing coach, Jim waits for each of his students to take their shot. This is the sort of pep talk Jim used to get me to write a poem at a session he offered at the NCTE meeting in Detroit (I hadn't written a poem since my undergraduate days).

Jim nurtures his family as much as he does his students. Jim and Eileen's children may be grown and married, but when I read his poems and listen to his stories, I'm sure he's still as devoted as ever to Brian, Tim, and Stacy, and now to his grandchildren, Ryan, Jessica, Liam, and the baby on the way.

One last revelation about Jim Mahoney. His favorite author is Robert Cormier, a former newspaper reporter and columnist who became the celebrated—and sometimes objected-to—author of such young adult classics as *The Chocolate War* and *After the First Death*. Jim likes Cormier for two traits he shares with British novelist Graham Greene: a staunch belief in morality—Cormier always makes one character in a story the conscience for the tale—and a style of using similes to describe people and places. But what Jim really likes about Cormier is that his gripping stories deal with adolescents—and that Cormier seems to understand and care for teenagers as much as Jim does.

So, after thirty-eight years of teaching and over a hundred workshops and presentations, most given with his friend Jerry Matovcik, this book is Jim's testimony to his passion for teaching young people, learning how to teach better, and helping new teachers and others who share his passion for learning. All that is left for me to say is, "Thanks, Jim."

JAMES STRICKLAND

ACKNOWLEDGMENTS
OR, WHO IS REALLY
IN CONTROL?

No speed of wind or water rushing by
But you have speed far greater. You can climb
Back up a stream of radiance to the sky,
And back through history up the stream of time.

Robert Frost,
"The Master Speed"

A NASCAR driver, in an interview not too long ago, was asked whether he felt he was in control of the car when he was racing. He responded quickly, "Heck, no! If I feel I'm in control of my car, I know that I'm going too slow to win." This book, as you will see, has a lot to do with who is in control and who is not in control. I wanted to relinquish some control of my students and allow them to race ahead to their literacy. As I prepare to send this manuscript to Jim Strickland, my editor, out in western Pennsylvania, my final task is to thank those who have been instrumental in bringing this book to the stage it's at.

Perhaps I should start with my seventh-grade teacher, Mrs. Sandiford, who ran a workshop setting in her classroom before we ever knew the term. She dubbed me "Sportswriter" and put me in charge of cutting newspaper clippings for a sports scrapbook. Mrs. Sandiford knew I liked sports and that I wanted to be a sportswriter like Dick Young of the *Daily News*, writing as he did about my beloved Brooklyn Dodgers.

Once, my very good friend Phil Bonasia whipped a piece of bubble gum at me from the front of the room and hit me in the eye. As I held my hands over my face in the middle of class, rubbing my eye, Mrs. Sandiford called out in a high voice, "Oh, Sportswriter," seeking to bring my attention back to the classroom. "Sportswriter, what's the matter? Take your hand away from your face and tell us what's wrong." Well, not in full control, I ratted on my friend, who was then pounced on by the very heavy, sparkling, blue-eyed teacher. Way back then, I had difficulty in discerning where my loyalties should be. Squealing on my buddy was the easiest way out. Now I've been given a chance to say who is responsible for this book, and I hope Mrs. Helen Sandiford, whom I hated at the time but came to admire years later, would be proud at seeing me as a writer.

"The Traveling Jim and Jerry Show." That's what our friend John Ferguson wrote when he described, for our brochure, the workshops that Jerry Matovcik and I have given for years on Long Island, in New York State, and occasionally at NCTE (National Council of Teachers of English) and CEL

(Conference on English Leadership). Who was in control of this show? My name came first in the billing, but it seemed that Jerry and I grew together, fed off each other, and learned from each other. Without Jerry, there is no me, and without me, there is no Jerry. Together, we pioneered our writing/reading workshop approach at the high school level. Neither of us is any more responsible for its success than the other. When one faltered, the other picked up the slack. When one doubted, the other reassured. On one day, one of us would take a poem or story, transform it into a powerful lesson, and give it willingly to the other. On the next day, the other would create a form to be used in class and share it willingly. When I couldn't make sense of something, Jerry could. When he stumbled, I found the meaning. Our mutual experience is too complex to capture here.

In 1990, we began this book together at the suggestion of several of our students, but we could never find the huge chunks of time we needed. Only after I retired from full-time work could I devote the necessary time to telling our story. While I have written the book, Jerry's work, spirit, and steady manner are present on all the pages. Well struck, Mr. Matovcik! Many, many thanks for the hundreds of hours together on our journey.

The other single most important person responsible for this book is my friend and close-up editor, Jim Strickland. I met Jim at CEL, actually ran against him for a position on the executive board but lost, and then listened to him encouraging me to put some of my ideas and practices onto paper. Over the years, Jim became a friend, then a confidant, and then a writing mentor. He was very active in writing and publishing several books of his own and in conjunction with his wife, Kathleen. But I was always reluctant to make the huge effort needed for such work, particularly when I wasn't at all convinced that any publisher would ever be interested or that any teachers would find what I had to say worth reading.

"There are already so many books on the subject," I protested to Jim in Denver in 1999. "But there are none in your voice and so you need to do it," he said simply. He asked me to freewrite on some of the things I was presenting and to send ten to fifteen pages along to him. Finally developing a determined stance, getting up in the dark each morning, I managed to send off about forty pages. Jim liked them and encouraged me to write more, so I left my consulting job as an interim department chairperson and began in earnest. I'd send off material and Jim would send it back all marked up with suggestions for revision, but he always found ways to help me keep going. Writing this book was one of the hardest, most demanding things I've done in my life. Jim gave me positive feedback but I just plodded along, determined to complete the task, believing that four or five friends and family members would be the only ones interested in reading what I had to say. After a while, I even began to doubt Jim because I felt he was so far into this with me that he had to keep encouraging me, just as I might do with a struggling student.

Finally, Jim sent out the first three chapters for review by folks in the field. Carol Jago and Jeff Golub both gave positive feedback—but they are friends of mine. Could I really trust them, or were they just avoiding being cruel? Paranoia was getting the best of me. Next Jim sent my chapters and Carol and Jeff's reviews off to Heinemann. Amy Cronin, acquisitions editor, read them and gave a positive response, then sent the chapters to Boynton/Cook's senior editor, Lisa Luedeke, who wanted to meet Jim and me to talk about the book. On a Saturday afternoon at the NCTE conference in Milwaukee, at the Heinemann booth, Lisa gave her approval. Jim introduced me to Maura Sullivan, Heinemann's marketing manager, who invited me to the Heinemann authors' reception at the Hilton that night. There I sat with Jim and Kathleen and Jeff Golub, watching the people whose books I'd read and whose workshops I'd faithfully attended as they came into the gathering. I was like a kid taken into the locker room of his favorite team to get autographs and meet the players. Of course, I was too shy to walk up to the likes of Don Graves, Lucy Calkins, Ralph Fletcher, Bill Strong, and a host of others and just join in the conversation. Instead, I admired from afar.

But the Heinemann people were so nice. Jim introduced me to Leigh Peake, the editorial director, and we talked, and then Maura came over with some others. Everybody seemed enthusiastic about my book. I could neither figure out why nor believe that it was all true and that the book would actually be published. When Amy Cronin sat down next to me, she told me how much she loved the first three chapters. As a former teacher, she said, she was touched by the story of the girl whose portfolio was lost and who offered a reward to the finder. She mentioned a number of other specific details and said that she actually cried over a couple of stories. She reassured me that Heinemann was highly selective about the manuscripts it handles. For the first time, I felt that what Jim and others were saying had some validity to it. Suddenly, I began to realize how hard it must be for students to believe in their own abilities— and that one can never get too much encouragement. It was only in the days and weeks that followed that my appreciation for Jeff, Carol, Lisa, Maura, and especially my editor, Jim, began to deepen. And I knew how hard it is for student writers to believe in their work.

I would also like to thank three people who worked behind the scenes at Heinemann. Eric Chalek did the initial legwork of making sure all the forms and figures and text matched up when the manuscript first arrived in Portsmouth. Eric was like Columbo, asking each time, "Just one more question. . . ." Vicki Kasabian, the production editor, guided me as well as the manuscript on each step of the journey, ever patient with my questions. Melissa Inglis, the editorial/production consultant, did a fabulous job with the proofing and revisions, a process that I feared would never end. She, too, showed patience and understanding. Thanks, Eric, Vicki, and Melissa.

I would be remiss if I didn't mention some of the many people who mentored me along the way. Several of these were father figures, older men to whom I could turn for advice in my younger years and who thought enough of me to include me in their circles. My greatest mentor and friend, my principal and fellow carpooler, my confidant, Ernie Tovo, died in June of 2000, suddenly. He was charismatic and all of his chairpeople flocked to his office after school to seek his company, to listen to his wisdom, to trade barbs with him. He helped me to be a better teacher and chairperson. I miss him dearly, and I can't thank him enough for all he gave to me, including helping me get to my first NCTE conference in 1981.

Other teachers of mine were Joe Heinlein, Jack Polo, Bill Gandley, and Bobby Dell. As administrators and coaches, they showed me how to teach or taught me "the game" and how to give it to my players. As a result, I began to see the connection between lessons on the field and learning in the class-room. Thanks, guys.

The English teachers at the Miller Place School District on Long Island tolerated my idiosyncratic ways when it came to my radical departure from the traditional approaches to the curriculum to a writing/reading workshop classroom. A few even embraced the change I was advocating. Teachers at the middle school and at the high school cared for and nurtured many of the students with whom I later had success. Maureen Sherer, Denise Helm, Stephanie Neil, Maryann Sommerstad, and other teachers seemed to have students in a writing/reading mode. Taking the students onward from there was easy. At the high school, John Newcombe became a dear friend as we shared the same room and many of the same philosophies. There would be times when Jerry, John, and I would sit and talk for hours after school, some-times joined by our friend Bob Budd, or by Ginny Crispell or others. The en-tire English department created an atmosphere that valued literacy. It was very comfortable working with the likes of Cathy Danowski and John Val-lone. My principals, too, supported me: Ray Sommerstad got me started and Dan Nolan gave me the impetus and trust to go further.

Nan Higginson, an English teacher at Miller Place, read the chapters on writing in their original draft form, chastising me for "having over a hundred pages in a single chapter on writing with no clear organization!" Using col-ored pens, this gifted teacher, editor, writer, and friend helped find some of the big ideas hiding in the dense material, providing some direction for re-vision before I sent it on to Jim Strickland.

Of course, my family has been both enthusiastic and patient as I've struggled through this project. My children know when they come in the house that I am probably at the computer upstairs. They wait for me to come down, but my grandchildren climb the stairs to see me and pull me out into the real world. How refreshing it is to be retrieved by a child, little or big. My children, Brian, Tim, and Stacy and their spouses, Trish, Debbie, and Chuck, have kept me buoyant, giving me topics and reasons to write.

And my wife, Eileen, has both tolerated this endeavor and encouraged it, just as she has always given me much space to grow in and in which to become whatever it is I am becoming. She has a way of making me feel good about my teaching and about my being a father. She tells me I have done a good job with our children. From Eileen has come quiet approval for this book. To her I give many thanks and much love.

So thanks, James, old buddy and editor, Eileen, Jerry, and all the rest for allowing me to get out of control occasionally in the search to tell this story of how I used a "speed far greater."

1 | TRYING TO FIGURE THINGS OUT

Janie finished her essay.
*   She never knew what grade she would get in Mr.*
Brylowe's English class. Whenever she joked, he wanted
the essay serious. Whenever she was serious, he had
intended the essay to be lighthearted.

Caroline B. Cooney,
The Face on the Milk Carton

My writing has changed. Then again, it changes every
year. English teachers as of yet have not yet converged
for a definite answer as to what they want in a well-
written essay, so I have to be retrained every year. By
the time I completely figure it out, "Oh, that's what
she wants!" It's June and the year is over.

From an eighth grader's portfolio

Lately I've been thinking about what makes the world go round. More and more, I see *power* as the central force. It seems that somebody wants someone else to do something or refrain from doing something. Somebody can be acting for good or evil; it doesn't matter. It comes down to whether somebody is going to win out or whether someone is going to withstand the force and not give in. It's all about power. Adam and Eve had a power struggle; Lucifer was cast out of heaven over power; and our human lives revolve around power. The struggle for power is also at the heart of most of the literature we teach. Parents deal with it and kids struggle to get away from it or to get control of it. Power plays a crucial role in schools—with students; with teachers; with building administrators, central office staff, the board of education; and with the community. Choose any aspect of school and see if it doesn't have something to do with compliance or taking away power: somebody exerting power by wanting somebody else to do or be something.

   In the first of the excerpts that open this chapter, a tenth-grade girl speaks about figuring out what will please the teacher. In *The Face on the Milk Carton*, by Caroline B. Cooney, the teacher, Mr. Brylowe, has power and wants Janie to do something—to conform to his writing assignment. The second quotation is a reflection from an eighth-grade student. Last June, I was helping the middle school teachers use a portfolio as a substitute for a final exam. The eighth graders had spent most of the year in a traditional classroom setting. They got teacher-directed assignments that were graded and returned with little conferencing and even fewer models of what the teacher actually wanted. This student was showing her frustration at the phenomenon she had conceptualized: being able to figure out what the teacher thought was good writing and then pleasing her by writing that way. Both the fictional Janie and my eighth grader had come to see that for the rest of their time in school, English would be like this: figuring out what someone else wanted.

It's the power issue. It's not that students don't want to become good writers or to compose their lives, or to discover the magic of writing so that they might explore and create. It's just that they keep getting different signals from their teachers. Teachers want students to become strong writers and readers, but too often they withhold the power to allow students to get there. And the problem is deeper than that. Even good teachers are so entrenched in the system that they don't see the problem at all. Many of them are trying to "figure it all out," to wrestle with the power they have but may not be using wisely. It is a lifelong process for teachers, but many lack the opportunity to go very far with their figuring because their school or department doesn't support such investigation. This book is an explanation of how I was able to go further with the help of my students and others. As students helped me, I was able to help them do the same. In collaboration, we discovered some truly literate classrooms.

The journey, though exciting, did not begin easily. It began for me on July 5, 1989. I remember being up in the middle of the night; I could not sleep. This was a rarity—I always sleep like a log. But Wednesday was to be the opening day of summer school, and I was tossing and turning because I had spent the last week, perhaps over sixty hours, planning how to turn over power to my students. I was a nervous wreck. I was preparing tc take a radical step with summer school students—kids who had goofed off all year and who had rightly failed. I decided that those who were making up for past sins by repeating the course would be able to choose their own topics and their own books; help in their own evaluations; and work without daily grades, quizzes, and tests. This was one of the scariest moments of my life, and I was wondering if I was committing career suicide. Perhaps in a few short days I would return to the well-organized, highly controlled class structure that had allowed me to be fairly successful for the twenty-five years I'd been teaching.

I was so nervous that I even scripted what I would say for the ninety-minute periods of English 11 and English 12 classes. In the past I had used lesson plans and improvised as necessary, going with the flow and working with whatever was available to make the material as meaningful to students as I could. But I had always been in control of what students wrote and read, of how they were graded, and of what they got to do in class and at home. The power was mine. Why was I planning to turn power over to my summer school students? What did I ultimately want from them?

I wanted what every English teacher wants. Most will tell you that they want their students to love reading as much as they do, which is often so much that their love of reading is the reason they became teachers in the first place. They may also say that they want their students to realize the power and the magic that comes from being able to write well. Rarely will teachers say they want their students to master subject-verb agreement, know the imagery of blood in *Macbeth*, or master the five-paragraph essay. Teachers want the big issues or the big ideas to stay with students. So why the shift for me?

The weather was brutally hot and humid that summer, beginning with that first day. But I was so ready that the students hardly had a chance to complain or even wonder. They began writing about themselves within the first ten minutes of class, and they wrote and wrote. They listed topics that they might develop in the future, modeled after a list I gave them. We told each other the topics we had so far and gave each other new ideas by sharing. The first forty-five minutes went by in the blink of an eye, and then I introduced reading choices to the students. I had the classroom filled with books that they could choose. I asked them to pick one that looked like it might be interesting. They went over to the bookcases, made one or two selections each, returned to their seats with the books, and started right in reading. Near the end of the class period, I explained that we would have no tests on any of these books but that we would be writing literary letters to each other about the things that struck us in the books. I asked the students to get a spiral notebook to write these letters in. I sent them home with either the book they had selected or the option to find a book at home that they wanted to read instead.

During the entire ninety minutes there had been no complaints, no requests to go to the bathroom, no disciplinary problems, and no students asleep with their heads on the desk. Not everyone was thrilled, but all of the students left having had a full class of reading and writing. They returned the next day with their books and notebooks, and I started right in with a minilesson on leads they might use in their writing. I introduced the "status of the class" report, in which all students report what they will be working on that day, and all of the writers went to work. At the end of the first forty-five minutes, we stopped writing. I began the reading half of the class with a minilesson on writing literary letters. In a second status of the class report, students told what books they were reading and how far they had read. I listed the titles and the pages they were on. While the rest of the class read, I met with individual students on the far side of the room. We talked about how their writing was going and what they needed help on. I was respectful of them as writers, and they respected the classroom atmosphere and the other writers and readers at work.

Slowly, during the course of the summer, their comments began to come: "Gee, I never really read a book before, but I like this when you can choose your own book." Or, "I like the kind of writing we're doing—you know, where you can write what you want and you don't have some dumb essay topic." Little by little, students began to see themselves as writers who had something to say and who could learn to say it in interesting ways. They began to report that they were doing a lot of reading on their own at home— and enjoying it. They wrote letters to me and I spent much time responding, first telling the students all the things I thought they were doing well and accomplishing that summer, then telling them my reactions to different things they had said about the books. For most students, it was probably the first time that they had ever received a personal letter in which a teacher treated them as a fellow reader. I loved the letters! Every time I got one, I felt as if the student were writing personally to me because he or she wanted to talk with someone about the book and I was the special one chosen. I felt validated by each letter and treated each one as if it were a gift. Though many students didn't yet have the skills to elaborate on a book the way I did, I never chastised them. Instead, I wrote long responses, finding much to praise about their ideas as well as about the book or the author. Just about every day was a treat for me, no matter how hot and humid the weather became.

It turned out to be a glorious summer. As the days progressed, I became more and more excited at what these so-called loser kids were producing. Kids who hadn't read a thing all year were reading. Kids who hadn't handed in more than an assignment or two in ten months were reading multiple books and were writing many papers that told of their lives, their struggles, their great moments. They acted like real readers and writers, talking to me and to classmates the way other readers and writers honor and respect each other and their work. Though the heat of summer raged on, the six weeks were delicious. Each day, I would give a minilesson then move over to a table near the window to meet with students about their writing. As the sun rose higher, a gentle breeze would sweep out of the woods just beyond the soccer field and blow into the windows, cooling and caressing me. Maybe I was delirious, but I couldn't get over how deeply I was getting to know these students, their reading and writing habits, what made them tick, and what troubled them. In turn, the students were accepting the power that I'd turned over to them and were finding themselves as fully engaged in school as they'd ever been.

My eleventh-grade students all took the New York State Regents exam at the end of the summer course, even though some of them came from districts where taking this exam was not a school requirement. The class also included students who were enrolled in resource room or special education programs, tracks that at that point did not even account for the notion that many of these students, given the right environment, could be successful on state tests. But special needs students that summer had been doing so much reading and writing for six weeks, more than most had done in several years of English combined, that they were all very ready to take this state exam. I took the last few days of class to prepare by showing them what the test looked like and how they could apply what they had been doing all summer to the tasks on the exam. They all passed, many with relatively high marks!

The students' responses as they completed the summer course were very gratifying to me. They bragged about how much they had written and read. They behaved like literate people who had done something worthwhile for themselves. I was euphoric. I had turned the power over to students and they accepted it and made something of it. I had asked them over the course of the summer what they wanted to learn and accomplish, and they had answered in interesting and diverse ways that validated my faith in their basic desire to succeed when given the option to do so. It seemed to me then, and I continue to believe now, that power was the central issue that we reckoned with in being successful. I figured something out by working with these students, and they in turn did their own figuring. All our success revolved around the chance to figure things out for ourselves.

LOOKING MORE CLOSELY AT THE POWER ISSUE

Another way of looking at power is to ask who controls what is taught in the classroom, when it is taught, and how students get feedback about their progress. That control falls into three areas that Nancie Atwell identified in *In the Middle* (1987): *time, ownership,* and *response.* Those three areas became the basis for the way I set up my classroom that first summer, and they have continued to be the foundation underlying my efforts to share power with students.

Time is a problem for most people. We never seem to have enough time in our own lives, and the desire for more time carries over into the classroom. We are always rushing to squeeze in just one more book or one more writing assignment or one more test. We think that if we had just a little more time, we would be able to do an even better job. How we handle time is a major issue for most teachers, so we view any interruptions of our time with great frustration. We have things to cover in the classroom, and usually it is we who decide how we will use the precious minutes. If we're not able to use classroom time well, students have to do their writing on their own time. We tell them, "We have too much to do and I have too much to teach you, so you can do that at home, on your own time." "Too much to teach" really means "too much to cover." However, students translate it as "I don't have time to teach you how to write or give you a chance to practice."

Imagine a basketball coach telling a team of poor shooters that he doesn't have time to work with them on shooting, an essential element of the game, because he has to introduce something sophisticated, such as a zone trap or an out-of-bounds play, to be used for the last few seconds of a close game. Such a coach would be emphasizing preparing for the outcome of close games over preparing for what happens during most of the time in the majority of games. One might argue about how the coach allocated practice time and whether winning the game was more important than teaching fundamentals that would carry over into other games and other seasons. But when it comes to reading and writing, teachers need to stress sound fundamentals over the less important things they might want to cover. Rather than occasional and unpredictable time to work on their homework assignment once the teacher has finished with the day's lesson, students need predictable, regular time in class to practice reading and to work with and talk with their teacher and their peers about their writing. Time is a power issue because decisions must be made about how much time will be given to things that need to be taught and learned. We need to examine how time is used.

Another power issue is *ownership,* or choice. Even if students are told that they can write about anything they want, there is still a problem: Often the teacher has already determined what form or genre they must write in— usually an essay—and what the piece's purpose, length, and audience will be—the piece will be written for the teacher and will be given a grade by the teacher. Our country was forged on the idea of freedom of choice in matters such as religion, governing officials, speech, and so on. But schools are often run like benign prisons. Generally the teacher determines what students will write about, what they will read, how they will be evaluated, and whether or not they have learned what they were supposed to learn.

From another perspective, we could look at how schools and teachers sometimes want to control students so they will realize the importance of learning. Most high school students really do want to learn and will readily learn if and when the activities are truly engaging. But the curriculum and the outcomes are determined without student input. Students see teachers and curriculum as their adversaries. To get students to comply, schools, parents, communities, and teachers use two forms of power: reward and punishment. Tests are used not to find out who needs what kind of help, but as a punishment when students do not perform as desired. Teachers foster this condition by saying, "Read this assignment tonight because there will be a quiz on it tomorrow." Such a threat seems to imply that the work is not much worth reading in the first place, or that students cannot see the worth of the assignment. Rather than addressing the problem, teachers skirt the issue by saying, "*We* know what's good for you. To make you take this medicine, I am going to punish you if you don't. You will get a bad mark if you don't do the reading and do it well enough to be able to answer my questions on the quiz." Students then ask, "What do we get if we *do* read the assignment well?" They are told that they will get a good mark on the test—and that if they do a good job on enough of these assignments, they'll be able to redeem their success in the future for admittance to a very fine college. And students who graduate from a very fine college are promised another carrot: They will be rewarded with many of the better goodies of the real world.

But there is a paradox about how much pressure students really need and it falls under the axiom "less is more." Richard Ryan and Jerome Stiller, two psychologists, elaborated this way:

> The more we try to measure, control, and pressure learning from without, the more we obstruct the tendencies of students to be ac-tively involved and to participate in their own education. Not only does this result in a failure of students to absorb the cognitive agenda imparted by educators, but it also creates deleterious con-sequences for the affective agendas of schools [that is, how students feel about learning]. . . . Externally imposed evaluations, goals, re-

wards, and pressures seem to create a style of teaching and learning that is antithetical to quality learning outcomes in school, that is, learning characterized by durability, depth, and integration. (Kohn 1993, 149–150)

Ryan and Stiller's findings can translate into curriculum issues as well as teaching methods and styles. In an effort to justify to myself that I was working hard as a teacher, I would sometimes work out all the things that students needed to do to succeed—on a test, with a particular project, or over the course of the year. In the way I used to teach, I supported the idea that students should have laid out for them exactly what was needed to succeed. I thus removed the opportunity for students to figure this out for themselves. My course outlines, my reviews for tests, and my whole approach were controlling, allowing for little criticism when students didn't measure up. I had laid out for them all the information for success, but I had forgotten to take into account learners' basic need to puzzle this through for themselves. In addition, I never had students participate in their evaluations, so they had to rely on my reward and punishment system being fair and my taking all the steps that would allow them to get rewards. This is what I used to see as good teaching, and this is what the majority of schools still rely on. Student ownership was missing.

The third power area is *response*. For a host of psychological and emotional reasons, we all seem to need feedback but we don't want to be evaluated or graded. What most of us want from others is to know what we did well and what needs improvement. Teachers seem to think that if they mark a student's paper and write a nice, encouraging note at the end, they are giving the writer the feedback he or she needs. Because the student produced the paper at home and with no help from the teacher, the teacher, who has so little time during school hours, in turn feels compelled to grade the paper at home and without the student present. The student gets a few quick moments in school to read the teacher's comments and the grade.

Most teachers would like to have the writer present to explain something quickly rather than having to write out explanations for writing problems, but because there is little opportunity to do this and so many papers to grade, teachers often resort to using short comments or symbols. Research shows that most students pay very little attention to the teacher's comments, either because "the game is over" once the grade is given, or because they can't figure out the teacher's cryptic markings and comments—and they don't believe they have any reason to do so. The response to their writing comes too late to be meaningful. Students see the teacher as the one with the power. If grades are important to them, they do their best to figure out and provide what the teacher wants. That's what Caroline Cooney's Janie and my eighth-grade student with the portfolio did. "Figuring it out," then giving it to the teacher exactly the way he or she wants it, is for many students to be the name of the school game.

In *Punished by Rewards* (1993), Alfie Kohn explains that unless people in the workforce have engaging activities and meaningful work to do, they turn to money for their satisfaction. In the passage below, I have replaced Kohn's references to money and work with references to grades and schoolwork so that we might consider whether high school students respond the same way adults do when they aren't given authentic and engaging learning experiences.

> Frequently, though, the quest for ever-higher [grades] can be interpreted as a symptom of a deeper longing. To listen to people who steer every conversation back to the subject of [grades], and who spend their lives grasping for more, is to speculate on what needs they are trying to fill with [academic] satisfactions. There is a tendency to focus by default on the size of one's [grade point average] when [schoolwork] is bereft of more important features: deprive someone of . . . genuinely engaging and meaningful [schoolwork], the capacity to exercise choice over what one does, social support, the chance to learn and to demonstrate one's competence, and that person will likely turn his attention to what [grade] he earns. (He may even dismiss as naïve the suggestion that [schoolwork] could ever be about more than [grades].) The same is true, as a number of psychologists and social critics have argued, when a sense of meaning or deep connection to others is absent more generally from one's life: a plump [grade point average] is made to substitute for authentic fulfillment. (132)

In the chapter "Lures for Learning: Why Behaviorism Doesn't Work in the Classroom," Kohn reports what Albert Einstein said of his experiences at Harvard. Einstein spoke kindly of his teachers but was critical of exams: "This coercion had such a deterring effect that after I had passed the final examination, I found the consideration of any scientific problems distasteful to me for an entire year" (151). If the threat of testing could have this much of an impact on a man who loved the subject matter of his field, we shouldn't be surprised that our students might falter, that after they jump through the intricate and demanding hoops we set up for them, many do not want to engage in any of the material ever again. Einstein only avoided his subject for a year. After all the forced reading we make high school students do, it's no surprise that when they are asked how they spend their free time, most list reading as one of the last things they would ever do.

One of the questions teachers and schools might look at is the extent to which they create "rigorous" conditions in the name of higher standards and academic excellence. Do schools help to foster those same Skinnerian attitudes of their graduates—responding like mice to external rewards—as they move on to higher education and then into the workforce? It is imperative for all thoughtful teachers to ask faculty to consider this issue on a school-wide basis. With or without the rest of the faculty, English teachers can take a radical departure from the system of rewarding and punishing students for their learning without providing them with helpful responses and having them participate in the evaluation process. English teachers can engage students in authentic writing and reading experiences. This book describes the many things I learned from students about how I could give them authentic experiences in the English classroom.

2 | THE PORTFOLIO— STARTING OFF

Everything starts with the portfolio. On the very first day of class, I pass out copies of portfolios from the previous year's students. I have students read the work and make observations about what they saw to themselves, to those around them, and finally to the class. I even ask them to turn to the back of the portfolio and write a short letter or note to tell the person who made the portfolio what they like about it. With this simple act, the circle of authorship ends for the previous year's students and begins for the new students.

GEARING UP

The afternoon sun of early April warmed the front of the room as I finished up a minilesson for my 11 Honors class. As I took some papers from the front desk, Caryn, sitting in the first seat, leaned in toward me and said in a low voice, "Mr. M, I am so psyched; I can't wait to start on my portfolio!" Her eyes were dancing and she clenched her fists in front of her as she went on, "I know exactly what I'm going to call it and I have the front cover all planned out. I'm so excited that I can't wait till we start. I have a whole pile of great pictures that I've been collecting for months. Mine is going to be the best this year, just the best!" You'd think a student (or teacher, for that matter) had been talking about school letting out and summer plans. But Caryn had done a portfolio in her 9 Honors class with my colleague Jerry Matovcik, then hadn't done one in 10 Honors. She was getting ready for what would probably be, in eleventh grade, her final chance to compose her life in a way that was meaningful to her. We had been talking about the portfolio since the first day of school, and since these students had done portfolios in ninth grade and had loved the process, they couldn't wait to do it again. Of course, not every student was as effusive as Caryn, but many were already champing at the bit, selecting paper, looking at various kinds of binders, thinking about what colors would work well on the cover. It reminded me of someone getting set to build a house and thinking about making every room special.

A day after my conversation with Caryn, Keri called me over to her desk and, looking through her wide glasses, whispered to me shyly that she was going shopping over the weekend with her mother. She said, "We're going to start picking out things for my portfolio and I need to know about requirements for the size or type of the folder or restrictions on types of paper. I don't want to get something and find I have to take it back." Keri had an outstanding touch for the most delicate detail in her writing and was anticipating making some of those finer touches in her portfolio. Keri and Caryn weren't eager beavers, unusual students simply looking to get work done early. This was only April and we weren't even into the fourth marking period yet. We wouldn't begin talking in detail about the final portfolio for at least five weeks. This portfolio would not be drudgery for me to announce, nor would it be hard to sell to the students. They were looking forward to it the way they might to the much-anticipated senior trip, to getting a learner's permit, or to going shopping for the prom.

And the excitement continued from these early days to the last days of school . . .

It is a Friday afternoon, the last day of school. Report cards were given out first thing in the morning. Students had received their copies of the literary magazine and the school newspaper, and all had departed within an hour. The teachers then attended a faculty breakfast, honored retiring teachers, listened to the principal give closing comments, picked up their final checks, and departed for the summer. Much of the school community will be getting ready for graduation on Saturday. But is now 2:30 and I am in the computer room with about twenty-five students and my buddy Jerry. These students, and some forty others who left recently, have spent the last several hours working on their portfolios. The report cards in their pockets record their final grades in English, so why are they still working on their portfolios?

STILL BUSY ON THE LAST DAY OF SCHOOL

"Don't anybody print!" The call goes out from a ninth-grade student who is standing over a printer. He has just put some designer paper in and is finally ready to print out a page on it. This cry has echoed through several computer rooms for the last four weeks, ever since we began the portfolio push. Students have been buying and trading fancy paper with each other for a while now and they are near the end of it, monitoring the linked printers to prevent other students from printing on their paper.

Nearby, several tenth graders are lined up to use the gigantic paper cutter I brought from my office. They realize that using scissors to cut out a picture for one of their pages "just does not cut it": A scissors-cut line will never be perfectly straight, no matter how steady the hand, so they use the paper cutter. Others see even better results with a utility knife and a straightedge. Once several pictures have been cut, off they go, picking up a glue stick to affix the pictures with a professional touch—tape or paste just isn't good enough for this operation. There is a constant hubbub as my radio blares out a song, some students singing the words while others make plans for the evening.

Jody Shenn is sitting at one of the Macintosh SEs in the computer room asking Colin McCabe how to make a particular design in PageMaker. He is finished with all of his writing and is finalizing his cover. We had talked in class about principles of layout, and Jody wants to have one set of boxes break into another. Colin is able to show him how and then return to his own work on the table of contents. They have some odds and ends to finish up before they hand in their portfolios and are on their way for the summer. They could have handed in something that would have been acceptable earlier in the week, but they've been poring over these collections for days now, wanting them to be perfect. Jody will soon be over to my table for me to give him the final pieces of Con-Tact paper for his cover and to put clear paper over the picture and title, the final stage before handing it in.

Behind me is Guambi Makoso, a ninth grader from Jerry's class. What is unusual is that Guambi is bent over his portfolio with his father, who came two hours ago to pick up his son. Guambi told his father he wasn't finished and that he would need several more hours. Mr. Makoso said that he would wait, so Guambi invited him to cut out pictures to accompany his writing. Father and son are bent over a page, sticking a picture below a reflection about one of the pieces of writing. Mr. Makoso looks up at the clock, sees that it is 3:00, and says under his breath to Guambi, "Oh, boy, Mom is going to kill us." Guambi goes to the gym to make a call to his mother to tell her where they are. Soon he comes back and asks me to come to the phone because his mother won't believe him. I assure Mrs. Makoso that her husband and son are indeed working on the portfolio and will be home within the hour. Actually, it will take them two more hours; they will leave at 5:00. Jerry and I are ready to leave too. It is the last day of school and most of the teachers left some eight hours ago. We will be in again on Monday to finish some work, but it's been a long, exhilarating week.

As I'm packing up, I think about the day and about the scene in the morning. On the last day of the year, students traditionally come in for just an hour to pick up their report cards, then get back on the buses and head for home. But I am also the advisor of the literary magazine, *Entre Nous*, and it has been a tradition for the last several years to give out the magazine on the last day of school, when staff members hand out the final edition of the school newspaper, *The Krob*. So many students have their work in the magazine that it was a quiet celebration as almost eight hundred students sat in their homerooms reading the poetry, prose, essays, and other works they and their fellow students had written.

Just before the staff handed out the literary magazine, my office was flooded with tenth and twelfth graders who had come to pick up their portfolios. I have cajoled many of them into leaving their portfolios with me so that I can use them during workshops Jerry and I will give for teachers. Others insist on taking their portfolios home to show their parents, but promise to bring them back the following week. Two of these are Jean Mathis and Casey Dean, tenth-grade students who, like so many of their classmates, created breathtaking work. They proudly picked up their portfolios and headed home, promising to return them once their friends and families had read them.

I recalled the last day of regular classes, two weeks earlier, when the tenth-grade portfolios were due and students filed in proudly with their finished projects. Many of them held up their prized possessions as they told stories of late nights spent poring over their work. Jean said that she had not been to bed all night. When I asked why, she said that she was so intently involved in all the little details of creating something she could be proud of that she just wasn't tired. Others chimed in that they hadn't gone to bed until 3:00 or 4:00 in the morning because of little things. It was not as if they had been goofing off and had procrastinated; they had been working for weeks each day in class or in the computer room, and at home as well. Just as a new highway or a building always seems to have a million little things to be completed at the end before the project is acceptable, most of these students found that their portfolios had many details to tie together, and they could not rest until they were done.

TIME: TAKE WHAT YOU NEED

In the last days of school, a handful of portfolios still hadn't been handed in. As in other aspects of student writing, time, ownership, and response are essential in the portfolio process. I had a policy that, although there were due dates, if students needed to, they could arrange for more time. However, they had to bring me the work they had done to show their progress. If I saw that they were continuing to forge ahead, I had no problem giving them more time. Usually, I could see that they were so far beyond a grade of A+ that I could simply put that grade on the report card and allow them to perfect their work.

Even if students came back two days later to ask for still more time, perhaps because of a problem with the computer or printer, as long as they showed me what they had done or told me about the problem, I would allow more time. I couldn't help laughing to myself sometimes when a student would hand in magnificent work three or four days after school had let out. That extra effort just made my summer reading so much more delightful.

OWNERSHIP: THE HEART OF THE PORTFOLIO— FIVE FINISHED PIECES

The heart of a portfolio is student writing: five finished, polished pieces. Over the course of the year, most students will write about twenty to twenty-five pieces, exclusive of literary letters. Some may even have more, but most have the required five or six finished pieces to contribute to their quarterly portfolios.

Although students include pieces from their writing during the year in the final portfolio, they also write many other pieces at the end of the year specifically for the final portfolio: reflections on the final pieces they've chosen, reflections on their writers' notebooks and literary logs, and "Dear Reader" letters introducing portfolios.

Some teachers, departments, and districts want to prescribe the genres that students' finished pieces cover. I can see the logic of that from the institution's point of view, but I don't find that students value the same things. It comes back to the individual portfolio: Whose portfolio is this? What is this portfolio's purpose? Is the portfolio being used to evaluate curriculum success, departmental or district progress, or individual teacher accountability? If so, the student's portfolio is being used for a different kind of final project and assessment than the goals I have. Perhaps the school or the teacher wants to be assured that every student is proficient in all of the genres. Although I don't think that any student has to be a jack-of-all-trades, requirements from certain genres can be satisfied during quarterly marking periods, and the pieces that satisfy them can be placed in students' quarterly portfolios. The final portfolio serves as the culmination of the year, but it is also each student's opportunity to *compose a life*, a phrase I use all the time with students to indicate that much of their writing is also a way of clarifying their lives and publishing this for themselves. They engnage in making sense of the big and small issues in their lives. Therefore, students should have a great deal of choice about which pieces are included.

At the risk of appearing to contradict what I just said, I do, in fact, ask that students have some specific types of writing in their final portfolio. Of the five pieces, one can be a poem. I don't want the final portfolio to be a poetry anthology. Using the portfolio that way might have been an option during quarterly marking periods, but in the final portfolio, students must demonstrate a range of skills and accomplishments. Another piece needs to be an example of expository (essay) writing. Sometimes this requirement might be even more specific: For example, students in my community college, 11 Honors, and senior English classes are required to include a literary analysis. I ask my tenth graders to do this type of writing but do not make the literary analysis a requirement of their final portfolios for these younger students. Some, however, choose to include it anyway.

One might ask why such a small percentage of the writing included in the final portfolio is expository writing, when most of the writing done by students in all school subjects is essays. Wouldn't it be more helpful to students to do writing in the forms they will use most in school? The portfolio is actually filled with other kinds of expository writing—at least eight reflections written for the portfolio, including students' reflections on their writers' notebooks and literary letters, and explanations such as "Dear Reader" letters. One astounding thing is that students always ask if they can put in more than the five required pieces of writing. During the year they have written between twenty and twenty-five pieces, and they value many of them enough to want to include them, going beyond what is required. Since this writing has already been completed and may be in a fairly polished form, it is often easy to include it. A feeling of "the more, the merrier" prevails, and before they know it, students are looking to make a packed portfolio even bigger because they still have more things they want to include. In theory, when I evaluate a portfolio and the five pieces that are worth 30 percent, I look for control of language, use of conventions, and full development. For the most part, students are very conscientious about making the pieces free from the errors that turn readers off: confusing sentences, spelling errors, run-ons and fragments, and other traditional taboos. We've discussed how others judge us based on aspects of writing that can be corrected with some diligence, and how failing to correct them is interpreted by readers as lack of caring for the reader's ease of reading.

OWNERSHIP: FIVE REFLECTIONS

In addition to five finished pieces, the final portfolios must include students' written reflections about those pieces. I ask students not only to "show me your stuff" in the final portfolio—to include "your best work and what's representative of the kind of growth you've made as a writer"—but also to explain why each piece is included. This is their chance to provide a guided tour of their work, to point out little things that they've done to enhance it. Some of this reflective writing has already been done as part of the quarterly portfolios. If students are careful about details in their quarterly reflections, they have some of the spadework for June's final portfolios done.

The handout on this reflective process (Figure 2–1) includes questions to prompt a variety of responses. Basically, I want to know what the piece tells about the writing craft and about the person. In the craft section, called "What the Piece Contains, Revealing the Skill of the Writer," I ask students to address the piece's origin, revision process, sentence structure, literary elements, organization, and composing process. The easier part of the reflection is the personal issues, "The Human Story Behind the Piece of Writing": the way the writer wants the reader to feel, the importance of the piece to another person, and the follow-up to the piece months later. All of these aspects are behind-the-scenes details, the kinds of things that audiences like to know about movie stars, sports heroes, and other people in the news. Teachers who read my students' portfolios, and other students and adults, often admit that they find a reflection to be more interesting than the piece itself. A reflection is even more within the writer's control than the original piece was, and the writer reveals even more of him- or herself in the reflection than in the original piece. These reflections count 20 percent toward the portfolio evaluation, so the required pieces and the accompanying reflections total 50 percent of the final grade. However, the students pay little, if any,

REFLECTING ON A PIECE OF WRITING
Reflecting, Not Rehashing

What the Piece Contains, Revealing the Skill of the Writer

A. <u>**Revision**</u>: Recall the stages that the piece went through to get to its current state—
   1. **Origin:** How did the idea for the piece originate? When? Where? Why? Who?
   2. **Transformation:** What feedback or self-examination was involved in changing this piece? A new lead, a recasting of sentences, adding information, deleting information, rearranging material?
   3. **Crafting:** What sentence structures have you used to enhance or present your material in the most meaningful way? Parallel structure, subordinating clauses or phrases, the absolute, appositive, participial phrase, two adjectives after the noun?
   4. **Literary Elements:** Have you used a figure of speech like a metaphor or a simile to get your idea across more fully or artistically? Have you used an analogy, an extended metaphor, the insertion of dialogue, stream-of-consciousness, flashback, foreshadowing, or other devices to help the piece?
   5. **Structures/Techniques:** What organizational features did you use for this piece? Did you use a lead of action, a series of stanzas in a poem, a two-part title, transitional words, a dialogue to present an issue or develop character? Why did you select these features?

B. <u>**Composing Process**</u>: How does the piece typify or depart from your usual composing process? How does it connect or depart from the kinds of things (topics) you usually write about? How is this a new area for you, perhaps a writing risk? What is your experience with this genre?

The Human Story Behind the Piece of Writing

A. <u>**Personal Importance**</u>: Why did you include this piece in your portfolio? What does it tell about you as a person?

B. <u>**Tone/Purpose**</u>: How should this piece be read or received? What voice or mood is to be conveyed during or after reading the piece?

C. <u>**Audience Reaction to the Piece**</u>: What kinds of responses have others had when reading this piece? Who? When? Why? Did the piece (**not the <u>events</u>**) have any lasting effects on you or on other people? Explain?

Creating an Interesting Reflection

Each reflection is very important because it is your chance to say why and how the piece reveals or presents your writing ability or what it has come to be. Here, you are the ambassador and the salesperson for the piece and for your skill as a writer. Therefore, each reflection should be carefully written, fully developed, and cover most of the areas listed above.

You ought to consider using a different font/size for the reflection and/or present it in a different format, such as in a shaded box or in some other interesting way.

FIGURE 2–1. *Reflecting on a Piece of Writing*

attention to this point value. They are interested in the development of the portfolio and not in what each part is going to earn them. One of the things we talk about is the value of making the reflections look different from the finished pieces. We look at magazine articles for guidance. Often, the commentary—the reflection—on an article is in a box or is shaded. Sometimes it's printed in a different font or italicized. These layout differences are important for the visual impact they have on the reader. Such shifts in appearance offer the reader the same kind of subtle guidance that paragraphing does in a written piece or that a switch in music does in a movie, signaling a change in emotion, point of view, or direction.

OWNERSHIP: REFLECTING ON THE SELF AS A WRITER

Though students are asked to think imaginatively about themselves many times during the school year, at the end of the year I ask them to use a metaphor to think of themselves as writers. This is another way of getting them to look at their composing patterns and habits. The handout "Thinking Metaphorically About Writing" (Figure 2–2) uses a number of prompts to help students to begin thinking of themselves and their writing habits imaginatively. This starts with thinking about how they write. Do they write fluently, or is it a slow and torturous process, like climbing a steep outcropping? Do they gush out words and pieces like a strong fountain, or do they dole them out one by one, like a gambler revealing his hand card by card? Do they find that they soar like a seagull during or after they compose? Do they find nuggets of gold in what they write, pawing through their words as a prospector would paw through a pan of gravel when he catches the shine? Key words like *soaring* and *nuggets* and *roaring* can suggest metaphors for students to use. They may see themselves developing like a river that inevitably makes its way down to the ocean, producing their writing in a meandering but steady way. Much is gained by stretching the imagination and seeing the ordinary in unusual ways. This process opens up new possibilities for seeing the world for the students at the same time it helps them look at the writing process in fresh ways.

    In addition to describing their writing process metaphorically, students look back in time to their development as writers, tracing their own writing trends from early childhood through elementary school to the present. They think about their struggles and successes and how they handled them. They wonder about their first writing and storytelling and look at how those things are linked with their reading development. They point to issues of punctuation as well as family reactions. They try to connect their present attitudes about the various genres they have written in with things they did in the past. If nothing else, they create a written record of their present-day perceptions and their origins. Such an account may be useful some day when they deal with their own children's literacy issues.

THINKING METAPHORICALLY ABOUT WRITING

1. Think of yourself as a writer or in the act of writing in metaphorical terms:

   I am **like a turtle** in my writing, slow and steady throughout the race. Unlike the others who sprint ahead with their ideas, only to get bored in a short time and lay their pens down, I stay with my idea, making small progress with my little feet each day until, at the finish line, I realize the great race I've covered and the work I've ground out, not dazzling but still pretty substantial.

   Writing for me is **like returning to a clear, cold mountain water spring**. As many times as I come back to this quiet little spot, I always get refreshed. Even the shady place is refreshing like the act of returning to my "writing shack." (running dry, bend over, put my face in, toad and frogs hopping around, bottom is clear but can easily be stirred up)

2. **Some Aspects of Writing**

   fears, problems, joys, habits
   where get ideas from
   how hold pen, body, paper, pen type
   place of writing, private, public
   how begin, develop ideas
   how revise, edit
   let others read? publish
   release feelings, clarify thoughts, tell stories

3. Use an act, an object, an animal, a profession. **Create 2–3 metaphors** about yourself as a writer.

   well, quarry
   hunting, running, mountain climbing
   migrating bird, chimp, a baby bird, a stallion
   sculpting, giving birth, coaching
   doctor, lawyer, sky diver, sailor

FIGURE 2–2. *Thinking Metaphorically About Writing*

A MINILESSON IN HONESTY

It's appropriate for me to include a few words about the honesty of students' reflections. Students are conditioned to give the teacher what they think he or she wants to hear. They don't believe they can be completely honest. This feeling creeps into the responses and reflections they write all year. Sometimes a student may write a literary letter to me extolling a book he is reading, but then in a letter to a friend state how much he hates the book and how he has given me "the old bull." If I see something like that as I glance through a student's literature log, I give a minilesson on truthfulness. I tell students that I am not upset by their saying how much they disliked a book, even a book that I may have recommended. I am upset, however, when they don't share their reactions so I can adjust my sense of what they like or are able to tolerate at that point. We talk about how to avoid hurting people's feelings while still telling the truth. The same is true for their reflections about the writer's notebook and the literary log. Some students think that I believe they will all love and relish every single thing they do in class. That is simply not true. I expect all kinds of reactions because of the individuality of students and because of my inability to minister successfully to each and every student. I ask students to make a statement about the issue, then explain why they feel that way. Despite these lessons and urgings, I can never erase the notion that students are trying to please me with what they write. It is for their own development, not mine, that I ask them to think reflectively about themselves and their work.

RESPONSE: REACTING AND RESPONDING TO THE PORTFOLIOS

As I head for my car on the last day of school, I have two big canvas bags full of 11 Honors portfolios that I will read at my leisure during the summer. I take them home because many students have asked me to write a letter of recommendation for colleges and I use the portfolios to talk about the level of each student's work. I read a portfolio or two each night in the summer, reveling in the work students have so magnificently done during the year and in the final weeks of school. I received the portfolios of my eighth, tenth, and twelfth graders a week or two before school ended, so I have had time to read their work, write some comments, evaluate the portfolios, and return them on the last day of school.

In late August each year, I make sure that I have the two bags of portfolios and my computer with me as my wife and I head to Hampton Beach, New Hampshire, for vacation. We stay for a week at a quaint bed-and-breakfast called the Victorian Inn. Each morning or each evening, I sit on the big porch of this old Victorian mansion, enjoy the breeze from the ocean just a few blocks away, and allow my students' images and feelings to mix with the lovely smell of the sea air. After an hour of my reading and making notes, my wife and I might head off for a day at the beach or some other adventure. During these lovely summer days my energy gets renewed by reading these portfolios and I again realize how privileged I am to receive such wonderful work. I have the time to respond in ways that students would appreciate.

THE REAL VALUE OF A PORTFOLIO—SHEILA'S STORY

A few years ago, I spotted a sign in the halls of Miller Place High School on the first day of school. The sign was repeated on walls on the first and the second floors, in the cafeteria, and in the library—everywhere throughout the building.

> $50 Reward
> Everyone could use a nice $50 reward.
> Be the finder of Sheila's lost portfolio.
> Name: Sheila Erimez   Portfolio Title: *Offerings*

Sheila's portfolio, the culmination of her ninth-grade English class with Jerry Matovcik, was so outstanding that during her tenth-grade year he and I would borrow it, along with those of other students, to show when we gave inservice workshops for teachers. The portfolios were always stored on a shelf in my office so that students could come in to get them or look at the comments that teachers wrote in the back during the workshops. The previous year's portfolios also served as models for our current students. The portfolios were in constant use. Unfortunately, Sheila's portfolio, which was kept with the rest, had disappeared on the last day of school. We couldn't find it at school or at our homes. When September rolled around, Sheila took it upon herself to post the signs around school, offering a reward of fifty dollars. She had wanted to offer one hundred dollars, but her father thought that the large amount might lead to some other problems.

The sad news is that *Offerings* never did turn up, despite rewards offered and closets emptied out. As she began a new year as a student in my 11 Honors class, Sheila was heartbroken, but she didn't let it get her down. She still had some of the pages on her computer and was able to reconstruct some of the missing parts, which she then included in her stunning new portfolio for eleventh grade, called *Canteen*. In this work, she eulogized the lost *Offerings* and connected that portfolio to some of the themes and pieces in *Canteen*.

While Sheila's loss had a more-or-less positive outcome, the larger point is the value of the work composed by a student. How many students would be willing to pay fifty or a hundred dollars for a copy of the Scan-tron answer sheet they had used for final exams? I can't imagine a single student wanting to even see the answer sheet once they know their final grade, never mind being willing to pay money to get the form back if it were lost. This incident illustrates the power of work that students view as meaningful. Essentially, most students come to see creating a final portfolio as a way for them to compose their lives at a time when the meaning of life is confusing for them. When they are fully engaged and are given time, ownership, and response, there is no end to the amount of time and energy students are willing to devote to their portfolios—or to the price they might pay to recover their lost work.

3 | THE NITTY-GRITTY DETAILS

Whenever teachers see my students' portfolios, they always want to know how the students were able to create such beautiful work. Naturally, teachers want the practical details, from how to make the covers and put the whole project together to how to find the time in school to get all the work done. This chapter describes how my students and I work together to create their portfolios.

GETTING PHYSICAL—CREATING THE PORTFOLIOS

The first year my students made portfolios, some planned to punch holes in their work and insert the papers into three-ring loose-leaf binders. Others planned to get clear plastic sleeves to insert into binders. Each sleeve holds two pieces of paper back to back, so each sleeve would have two views, the front and the back. But I decided to try a method my classes had used earlier in the year to make cardboard covers for collections of poems we entered in the Walt Whitman Poetry Contest on Long Island. I used a desktop publishing program to place all the students' typed poems onto pages, then made a cover the way I had learned from Melissa Conlon, a student from two years before, who had learned it from her mother, an elementary school art teacher. Melissa had written a children's story and had bound it with a hard cover. The book won first prize in a contest on Long Island. Inspired by Melissa's success, Taras Kootz, in Jerry's 9 Honors class the following year, created a children's book. We helped him lay out pages on the computer before he took the material home to bind it. His sister Orycia, who had been in the same class as Melissa, remembered how to bind books; however, she made another refinement—wrap the cardboard cover with Con-Tact paper, then attach a picture and title to the front cover. The result was a beautifully bound book for Taras—and another first-place award.

I needed to make covers for four class anthologies. After printing the ten to fifteen pages of poems for each anthology, I placed blank pieces of paper on top of the first and last printed pages. Then I stapled the pages together down the left-hand margin, with the staples about an inch apart. Using a utility knife and a straightedge, I cut two pieces of cardboard a little larger than the 8 1/2-by-11-inch pages of the anthology. As shown in Figure 3–1, I laid the two pieces flat side by side, with a slight space between the two long edges so the cover would close once papers were inserted, then used packing tape to tape them together. I then used Con-Tact paper, cut about three inches longer than the two covers opened up, to cover the cardboard. After some trial and error, I learned how to put the Con-Tact paper on smoothly. I placed the stapled pages down and used packing tape to affix the pages to the inside of the cover on the front and the back. I then took a solid tan colored sheet of Con-Tact paper and placed it on the blank top (first) page and smoothed it down by pulling it left across the page and onto the inside of the cardboard cover. I flipped the pages over to the back cover and did the same thing. The result was that the pages of the anthology were securely attached inside the cardboard cover, and the front and back inside covers had a piece of neutral colored Con-Tact paper to cover up all the staples and tape. The inside of the cover looked almost like the inside of any published children's book.

I used the computer to create a cover sheet, writing the title and other information and leaving space for a picture that I'd cut out of a magazine. I printed it out on designer paper, used a glue stick to attach the picture to it, and then attached it to the front cardboard cover on top of the Con-Tact paper. Finally, I used a sheet of clear Con-Tact paper to cover the whole front so the cover would be protected from dirt. The outcome was four stunning-looking books of student writing. (Incidentally, each of our class anthologies won first prize in its grade level. Who says you can't judge a book by its cover?)

Because students were so impressed by the portfolio cover I was making, a few asked if they could do their portfolios the same way. As we worked on the covers in class, many saw what other students were creating and wanted to do the same thing. By the time the year was over, all but about five of my ninth-grade students and all but four of my twenty-three seventh-grade students had constructed their own portfolios using cardboard and Con-Tact paper. I discovered that taking home these cardboard portfolios was much easier than carrying home a pile of bulky, heavy loose-leaf binders. I also thought that the work in the cardboard portfolios was of higher quality than the work in the binders. The students seemed to see the cardboard portfolios as more personal and more important to them, which seemed to inspire them to make their writing more personal and important, too.

Mass Production in the Classroom

Right about now, a high school teacher reading this must be thinking, "What is this guy talking about? Con-Tact paper? Cardboard cutting? This is for art class. I've got literature to teach!" Yes, creating the portfolios may seem to be stealing valuable classroom time, but I offer testimony from students who became obsessed with working on their writing and with the process of

Making a Children's Book/Collection of Writing

1.

| pages of your book |

Needed: The pages of your book plus two cover sheets, front and back.

1. Pages are stapled together.

2. Cut 2 pieces of cardboard, 1/4 inch larger all around than pages.

3. Tape down the center of the cardboard on both sides, front and back, but make sure to leave a 1/4 space between the covers so the book will close.

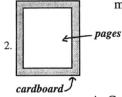

2. — *pages*

cardboard

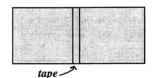

3.

tape

4. Cut paper for cover (wall paper or contact paper) 1/2 inch larger on all sides than size of book. Glue paper to cardboard. One side will be covered.

Note how "contact" paper is cut off on corners

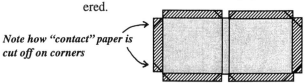

4. & 5.

5. Fold cover paper over cardboard and glue with rubber cement.

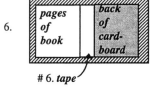

6.

| pages of book | back of card- board |

6. *tape*

6. Place book on center and tape both sides to cover.

7. Take either the same material as on the outside cover (wallpaper) or some other material (even plain white paper) and cover the inside front cover and the first page of the book. Flip the pages over and do the same with the back cover and the last pages. Glue these on with rubber cement. The cover sheets will overlap the paper that was turned in. (See step 5.)

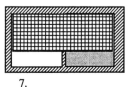

7.

8. Open each page and carefully flatten slightly.

FIGURE 3–1. *Making a Children's Book/Collection of Writing*

putting their portfolios together. I believe that they wouldn't have had quite the same intensity had they not been involved in creating the containers their portfolio work was to be placed in.

I'll always remember one very bright student in my 11 Honors class, Aron Erimez. While other students in the class were choosing pieces to include in their portfolios and deciding which themes might appear on various pages, Aron spent days on his cover. He wanted the cover to have a square cutout that the title showed through. He spent hours on his title, running it through the laser printer and then putting an overlay of gold foil on the print, an embellishment he had learned when we made pieces of writing as gifts. Aron mounted the title behind the hole he had cut in the front cover. Using a piece of dark red velvet cloth, he wrapped the cardboard cover front and back, then added the title *Velvet Offerings*. The portfolio he eventually produced held one beautiful page after another. Despite my frequent urgings that he move on to more important things, Aron had to work from the cover to the portfolio, not the other way. One lesson to be learned from this is that if we want students to produce their best work, sometimes we have to be patient with the way they go about doing it. But I digress.

When I told students to bring in pieces of cut cardboard and the kind of Con-Tact paper that they wanted for their covers, all kinds of problems arose. Cardboard comes in a variety of thicknesses, from refrigerator crates to cleaners' shirt backings. In addition, some students had no skill at cutting cardboard straight. Some tried to cut with scissors. Others used a utility knife but didn't use a good straightedge. Some couldn't find any Con-Tact paper in the stores around their homes. Frustration reigned.

What could I do to help the many students who wanted to make portfolios that looked like those class anthologies? I began by asking them to bring in all the cardboard boxes they could find, including those from supermarkets and other stores. They broke the boxes down and piled them in my office. I brought in several utility knives, several short T squares that I had at home for cutting plasterboard, and a three-foot-square piece of plywood for cutting on. Using my free periods and time after school, I cut the cardboard into pieces approximately 9 1/2 by 12 inches. Then I purchased rolls of Con-Tact paper in a variety of colors and shades, including clear, to use for the final covering and solid colors for the inside covers. I told my students that they had the choice of purchasing their cover materials themselves or of getting all the cardboard and Con-Tact paper they needed from me for two dollars. As the year came to an end, when students seemed to rely on me less for writing conferences, it was not unusual for me to be in the front corner of the room with a group of students putting together covers, helping with Con-Tact paper or attaching text pages to a cover. I wasn't doing the work for them. They always had the sense that they were making their portfolios themselves, under my direct supervision.

While some students made portfolios, others might be upstairs in the computer room. Some students might be across the room completing the work for the fourth quarter, reading their current book, writing a literary letter, or answering a letter. If the majority of the class needed to go to the computer room, we would all go together. I would carry my bag of Con-Tact paper, my plywood, and my tools up to the desk in the front of the computer room and work from there. When we did this, students never seemed to have a problem concentrating on their computer work, even though others might be talking with me about their portfolio progress as they measured, cut, glued, picked out Con-Tact paper, and did other activities related to their covers.

Design Improvements

One problem with our portfolio design was that after stapling all of their pages together and attaching them to the cardboard covers, nothing short of reconstructing the portfolio could be done if a student discovered a major mistake on one of the pages or realized that a page had been left out or put in the wrong order. To solve this, someone came up with the idea of using the plastic sleeves made for loose-leaf binders and attaching those inside the cardboard covers. This allowed the students some leeway in calculating how many pages they would have and enabled them to take papers out or switch them around if they so desired. That year, most of the portfolios were made with plastic sleeves inside cardboard.

Then we discovered presentation folders, which are made of sturdy but flexible plastic covers and attached plastic sleeves. The preferred model has twenty-four sleeves, which lets students insert forty-eight pages back-to-back. A similar folder that uses about twenty small plastic rings to hold the sleeves in lets students add more pages if their portfolios grow beyond forty-eight pages.

Some models of presentation folders have a plastic pocket on the front cover for inserting a title sheet or cover page. This seemed to be exactly what teachers and students needed, but I sensed that the charm of the old portfolios with their hard cardboard covers and their Con-Tact paper would be lost to conformity. I began experimenting with taping pieces of cardboard to the presentation binders, then applying Con-Tact paper to these new covers. The resulting portfolio looked like a high school yearbook or a hardcover book, but still had the flexibility of the plastic sleeves. I showed students the prototype I was working on for the Walt Whitman Poetry Contest, and as we created several poetry anthologies this way, students began to use this method for making their portfolios. Once students had their portfolios covered with Con-Tact paper, they began to fill them with the pieces they were revising. After designing and printing a cover page, they brought the portfolios back to me to help them glue the title page onto the front cover and seal it with clear Con-Tact paper.

As I had done previously, I told students who had trouble getting portfolio materials that I would pick up folders for them if they gave me the money, since I went past an office supply store every day on my way home. For $5.50, I would get the binder for them. For another $2.00, they could get the cardboard and all the Con-Tact paper they needed. Some students brought in their money right away. Others waited before deciding. A few used old three-ring loose-leaf binders. While there was no penalty for choice of portfolio, it seemed to me that the students who chose a plain loose-leaf binder were not as involved in the portfolio process or in their schoolwork in general as the students who created their own portfolios were.

Page Design

We used designer papers to print portfolio work pages on. The younger the students were, the wilder the paper that they chose: They used images of lakes and their reflections, images of the American flag, soccer ball borders, and many other kinds of colorful displays. Sometimes students would get together to buy special paper from stationery stores or mail-order companies, then would divide it among themselves. I helped by buying large supplies of designer paper and offering it for five cents a page. If someone needed just two sheets of a particular paper, they could get just what they needed for a dime.

Students chose their designer papers carefully. Those in the upper grades thought that changing from one designer paper to another on every other page was tacky. Some noticed that using off-white paper throughout the portfolio could look far more elegant and sophisticated than using plain white paper. We talked about layout principles and examined professional publications as models. Students noticed that the placement of text on the page; the use of a consistent design element, such as a repeating line on each page; or the use of a shadow or a box could be far more effective than using colorful but busy designer paper. Each year the students grew more conscious of the visual effect of their portfolios.

"Does Anyone Want Pizza?"

As advisor to the literary magazine, I often suggested pizza for our Friday afternoon work sessions. And as the benefactor, I chose the pizza place. I grew to like one particular place—Matt's Pizza. When we finished the pizza, I took the boxes downstairs to my office. One day, I looked closely at the cardboard and thought that it would make a great portfolio cover. It was just the right thickness, and it didn't have the ridges that create a corrugated look when you apply solid black Con-Tact paper to some cardboard. Matt's Pizza boxes were white on the outside and very smooth. Every time we had pizza at school or at home, I saved the boxes. I think that sales of Matt's Pizza went up as I spread the word. Some students swore that they could detect a hint of pizza if they pressed their noses close to their portfolios, but I told them that it was only their imagination.

PORTFOLIO TYPES

There are basically three types of portfolios: *showcase, growth*, and *limited*. Jerry and I had the best success with showcase portfolios. These contain students' best final products presented in showcase style, using pictures and designer papers as well as paying attention to layout and other design aspects to make them visually appealing. Many students love this type of portfolio and are willing to work hard on the writing that will go into it.

A growth portfolio asks students to show their growth in writing over a period of time by including examples of weak early writing along with writing that shows their improvement. The samples might include handwritten drafts of work in various stages. Such portfolios are harder to evaluate than showcase portfolios, and are not as attractive to students or outside readers.

Limited portfolios might require all students in a grade to include a particular type of assignment, such as a personal narrative or a literary analysis. These collections might be nothing more than manila file folders that hold the required assignments that students consider their best. Such requirements are generally district- or state-driven and are used to evaluate programs rather than students. They limit students' choice and take away much of their incentive to compose their own lives through their portfolios.

My students' final portfolios come out of a workshop setting and use quarterly portfolios as staging points. This system has a flaw: When portfolio assessment options are available to teachers, and particularly when they are mandated, abuses will creep in, such as assigning a portfolio and not giving students adequate class time to work on it. Sometimes teachers still want to "cover" more work and so they make the portfolio a homework project that students then see as an additional burden. These actions will kill students' enthusiasm. At Miller Place High School, we switched administering the state exam in English, called the Regents exam, from June to January (a choice given to all districts) so that the second half of the junior year could be devoted to creating a portfolio. However, when we switched to January and required a portfolio of all students, some teachers created more work for students at the end of the year. Students, whose teachers didn't value giving up class time for some of the portfolio work, came to see *this* kind of portfolio creation as less than joyful and more as a chore. Mandating portfolios sometimes results in abuses.

I found that the eleventh graders who had done portfolios for a few years before reaching my class were eager to repeat the process, not turned off by it. No one ever said, "Oh no, we have to do that again!" As a matter of fact, we talked in class about how students felt about their earlier portfolios. Some said that when they were younger they had thought that their portfolio was simply the greatest, but as they looked at it from an older student's vantage point, they saw both the subject matter and their tastes in design and layout as being very immature.

Other students had a nearly opposite reaction. They knew that they had grown and that their tastes and skills had changed, but they still cherished the earlier work because it was honest and represented their best efforts at the time. These discussions allowed the students to rediscover how and why they had been the readers and writers that they were at a much younger age.

"STUDENTS ARE TAKING THESE PORTFOLIOS TOO SERIOUSLY!"

After I left Miller Place High School, a problem with the portfolios that I had seen coming developed in full force. The chairpersons of several departments requested that work on student portfolios be curtailed or done before the final class days at the end of the year. The students were so obsessed with the construction of their portfolios that they were not putting adequate time into their other subjects. As a result, they were not well prepared for their final exams and were not producing the expected high scores. Never mind that this wasn't true of all students in grades other than eleventh, since at least half of the English teachers used paper-and-pencil final exams instead of portfolio evaluation: Too many students were so engaged in their portfolios that they spent "inordinate" amounts of time on them, often working late into school nights and occasionally not even sleeping.

One of the best portfolios I ever received was done by one of the five most gifted and hardworking students I ever had. *Allure*, created by Alan Lemley, was simply outstanding. When Alan handed his portfolio in during testing week, I was immediately struck by the quality of his work. When I actually read it and saw how he had connected all the pieces and the reflections, I was awestruck. Tucked away at the very end of the portfolio was a comment made to no one in particular:

> While creating this portfolio, my grade became a secondary consideration. I was interested in collecting my work so that I could be proud of it—when I show it to others and when I look back at it in the future. Stated more clearly by Frost, my final portfolio is an application and proof that I have used "speed far greater."

Alan was referring to Robert Frost's poem "The Master Speed," which he had placed in the portfolio next to his own poem imitating Frost's style. Alan was also saying what so many other students had said and would say over the years: When given the time and the opportunity to choose, students will spend uncountable hours without any thought other than the fascination of the work. External rewards, which they sometimes assume will be a grade of A, are not the driving force. It is composing themselves in words and images that matters.

WHAT GOES INTO A PORTFOLIO?

One of the first things that some students want to know is what is required in the portfolio. This is a fair question, particularly for students who work best by understanding the whole process from the beginning. Figure 3–2 is

Name of Portfolio _____ Name _____

Final Portfolio Grading Sheet — English 8

Points

1. **Dedication, Acknowledgments:** awareness of publications, presentations (3) = _____
   5) great   4) very good   3) much   2) some   1) little

2. **"Dear Reader" Letter:** Depth of invitation/ purpose, explains
   theme/cover   (7) = _____
   5) fully   4) very much   3) much   2) some   1) little

3. **Table of Contents:** Shows organization of materials and page numbers (3) = _____
   5) great   4) very much   3) much   2) some   1) little

4. **Reflection on Lit. Log/Best Literary Letter w/ Response, and Record** (7) = _____
   of Books Read: retyped, reflective, examples
   5) fully   4) very much   3) much   2) some   1) little

5. **Five Pieces of Writing:** level of work, attention to detail, developed,
   edited   X (6) = _____
   5) fully   4) very much   3) much   2) some   1) little

6. **Reflections on the 5 Pieces:** story of each piece, writer's skills in
   ea. piece/feelings about pieces, writer as a person/why included X (4) = _____
   5) fully   4) very much   3) much   2) some   1) little

7. **Reflection on the Writer's Notebook:** developed/specific. Examples (7) = _____
   of how the notebook was used, how the use changed or got altered
   5) fully   4) very much   3) much   2) some   1) little

8. **Biographical Poem/Sketch of Writer w/picture:** gives interests, talents, (5) = _____
   aspirations
   5) great   4) very much   3) much   2) some   1) little

9. **Cover:** cover, title—care taken in arrangement, selection of title, (8) = _____
   appearance of cover:
   5) great care 4) very much   3) much   2) some   1) little

10. **Arrangement and Layout of Pieces of Writing:** thought and care
    given to the appearance and presentation of the writing, use of pictures. X (2) = _____
    5) great   4) very much   3) much   2) some   1) little

General Comments:

Grade _____

the eighth-grade version of a final portfolio grading sheet that, with modifications, I've given to students at all levels from middle school to first-year college. The number of requirements in the handout vary slightly depending on the situations and conditions, such as grade level, ability level, curriculum requirements, and time constraints, but the basic philosophy remains the same: At the heart of the portfolio is the fact that students are composing an account of their life. The grading sheet lists the elements that students' portfolios must contain. The paragraphs that follow discuss several of these elements. Other elements—Five Pieces of Writing, Five Reflections on the Five Pieces of Writing, and Reflections on the Writer's Notebook (the self as writer) are discussed in Chapter 2.

Dedication, Acknowledgments

Students experience a sense of pride and accomplishment when their own portfolios are finished, and they also often realize they have benefited from other's hard work. Students help each other proofread pages and create layout features, inspire and encourage each other, and share paper and other materials with each other. Many students recognize that they might not be who they are without the love and support of parents or family member, boyfriends or girlfriends, teachers or guidance counselors, or someone else who played a key role in their life. Students express their debts to others on an acknowledgments or dedication page in their portfolios. We talk about being honest with these dedications and acknowledgments, because they could be hurtful if done thoughtlessly. Parents, when a work is dedicated to them, become genuinely touched and have said they've felt closer to their child then they've felt in a long time. Some students place their dedications first in the portfolio, before the title page. Others want their title page to be first in the book, on the right-hand side when the book is opened, so they place their dedications on the second page, on the left-hand side, following the title page.

The "Dear Reader" Letter

The idea of students using their portfolios as a "letter to the world" came from a National Endowment for the Humanities (NEH) seminar on the works of Walt Whitman and Emily Dickinson that Jerry and I attended. In her poem #172, Dickinson wrote "This is my letter to the World / That never wrote to Me—" (103). We saw this poem as a desire to have some response by the world she was writing for but which would never have the chance to write back to her. With Dickinson's letter to the world idea still fresh in his mind, Jerry came up with the idea of having students write a letter to their readers, asking them to write back with their reactions to the work. The readers the students write to are anyone who might read their work—their own teachers; their parents, close friends, and classmates; the teachers who see the portfolios at the conferences and workshops that Jerry and I give. The "Dear Reader" letter explains what is to be found in the pages of the portfolio and its importance to the writer. It might even mention the significance of the portfolio's title and how it represents an aspect of the portfolio's theme. The letter might also ask for honest feedback, or invite a reader to sign the back to indicate who has stopped for a "visit." The two examples that follow show the range of our students' letters to the world.

Kerri's letter.   Some letters, like Kerri Bianchet's, aren't highly detailed. The "Dear Reader" letter Kerri wrote for her portfolio, *Daydream Believer,* included a poem.

> Dear Reader,
>
> > With your two eyes you can see into the world
> > With your hands you can feel what I feel
> > But with your body, mind, and soul combined,
> > You can enter into my personal thoughts,
> > Taking a piece of me with you,
> > And leaving a piece of yourself with me
> >
> > Take your hands and leave me a memory
> > Written down in this book.
> > Your feelings can mold mine,
> > And together new pictures can be
> > Formed for future endeavors.
>
> With this thought I invite you to travel through the pages that follow, bearing in mind that on each page a piece of my soul is left behind. Those who do not know me well may be surprised with my pieces, and those who know me might be stunned. Yet please do not joke or laugh about them, for each one was created from a separate thought, memory, or feeling. Instead, let the words travel to your soul and allow them to make you laugh, cry, remember, or even become your own daydream believer.
>
> However, before you close the cover to this book, please leave your name, as well as any and all comments—I will accept your criticism and love your encouragement. Whatever your feelings may be, your words will help me continue to create, dream, and believe.
>
> Yet, first and foremost, enjoy your journey through this *Daydream Believer.*
>
> > > > > Love,
> > > > > Kerri Bianchet

Jeff's letter.   Some letters, like Jeff Heckelman's, are more detailed. Jeff points out all the divisions in his portfolio, titled *Into the Void*, and personalizes the avoid. He begins with a definition of the word *void*:

> **Void** (void) n. **1** An empty space; a vacuum. **2** A breach
> of surface or matter; a disconnecting space.
> **3** Empty condition or feeling; a blank

To those who may discern,

There is a void in each of us. It may be a place we dare not go, or a distant euphoria towards which we endeavor to strive. Nonetheless, a void it is, and a void it shall remain unless it is filled in some way. Thus is the meaning of this collection. In creating these works, I have filled part of a void in myself, and in giving them to you, I hope to fill a void inside you as well.

For me, the void is not a dark place. I have had darkness in my life; therefore it is not an emotion I feel I need to experience again. This void is one of reflection and celebration. I have taken this time in my life, a crossroads, you might say, to look back on the path of life that I have taken thus far. In doing so, I have realized that while I've had some tough times in my life, they have served to make me an even stronger person, and I can now say that I am a happy, content individual. There is much that I strive for, and I see no end for my hard work in sight, but as yet in my life, I have no regrets. Thus, my void is nearly full.

I say nearly full because if it were completely full, I would have nothing more to strive for. As I said, in creating this, I have partly filled the void. I hope to fill it some more with the effect it creates in you, gentle reader. Nothing would give me greater pleasure than to see my writing have a positive impact on another life.

I have chosen to divide this book into three sections: poetry, prose, and miscellaneous creations. I have done this for a very important reason: each represents a different aspect of me as a human being, therefore filling different voids. My poetry represents me at my reflective best. I celebrate the things I love in my poetry: my family, running, baseball, and love itself.

I reflect in my prose writing as well, but in a different way. When I write prose, the reflections are often in the work itself. As you will notice, none of my prose pieces have a corresponding reflection. This is because I feel that my prose writing requires no added explanation. It speaks for itself.

In the "miscellaneous creations" section, you will find just that. Pieces that have no other place in this anthology—they have minds of their own. You will encounter my brief foray into the world of parody literature, an analysis of a poem, examples of literary letters to peers and teacher alike, as well as reflections on myself as a reader, my literary log, and my writer's notebook.

I implore you, gentle reader, to step into my void. Here, there lie things that you have never seen before, and things you will never see again. Step into my void and bring your friends. Let's see how many it takes to fill it up.

Deliberately yours,
Jeff Heckelman

Table of Contents

A portfolio's table of contents is easy to do, but must wait until the end. While a table of contents is not entirely essential to the reader of the portfolio, who generally reads the work from first page to last and rarely needs to look up a particular item, having the student do this page gives a broader view of the whole collection. Getting this sense of perspective, as you might get from walking back to admire the first freshly mown lawn of the spring, then allows the opportunity for the student to place page numbers on the individual pages and solidify them in the table of contents.

As simple as creating tables of contents is, the students and I look at real books to see how other authors have done it. This continues to reinforce the concept that the students are doing what real writers do, giving authenticity to the task. I've seen portfolios that were little more than manila folders holding a collection of the student's writing. Such portfolios have none of the trappings of the work that real writers do. When you remove some of those seemingly insignificant trappings, you remove the aura of authorship. Even a table of contents is important.

Reflection on Literature Log/Best Literary Letter with Response

Since students are creating a literacy portfolio, they are asked to include literary letters and reflections from their literary logs to show the gains they've made in reading and literature study as well as their growth in writing. During the year, students write some thirty-five to forty literary letters to their peers, me, and other adults, including their parents, other teachers, student teachers, and family members. The people who receive the letters write back to the writer in the same literary log that was given with the letter in it. I ask them to select and type up two or three of their letters and the accompanying responses to include in the final portfolio. Students usually include photocopied excerpts of other authors' work when they write literary letters in their spiral notebooks. For the portfolios, I show them how to format text to make it clear it's an excerpt: Indent it on both margins, reduce the font size, and lessen the leading (the space between lines). Students then retype their handwritten letters, including the formatted excerpts from other authors' work.

In addition to literary letters, students also include reflections in which they examine themselves as readers. This lets them take a long-distance view of their reading growth. The end of the year is not the first time students look back on their work. At the end of each quarter, they write a reflection in their literary logs about the reading they've done and the literary letters they've written. In the first quarter I hand out "A Backward Glance: Reflecting on the Writer's Notebook and Lit. Log at the End of the Quarter" (Figure 3–3). This form lists questions for students to ask themselves about the work they've done during the previous ten weeks. When they write about their use of literary logs at the end of the year, they must page through one or two notebooks they've filled, rereading their work and examining their thinking at the time. I ask them to look for trends in their reading, their thinking, the kinds of letters they wrote, and the literary genres they gravitated toward. I want them to take stock of their own reading habits, skills, and interest levels.

Some students write good responses in literary logs and others don't. Sometimes the response depends on the book, but usually it has to do with the level of reflective thought that the student invited peers (the ones receiving the letters) to participate in. When the writer of the letter only summarizes a book, the responses are briefer; when the writer asks readers what they think of a situation in the book and how it applies to their lives, the responses are more thoughtful and detailed. From reviewing their literary logs, students realize that they get more interesting replies when they make real efforts to engage their readers.

The final portfolio's reflection on the literary log also asks students to chronicle their growth as readers from childhood. Some have been lifelong readers of a variety of texts; others stopped reading near the end of elementary school or when they got into middle school, even though they might have been read to as children or even have been avid readers through third or fourth grade. By taking this look over time, students begin to see what kind of readers they've become, who their favorite authors are, and what genres they like most. Such self-assessment is more valuable to students than the mere 10 percent it is worth to the portfolio grade.

Rob, a prolific reader and a student with great wit, wrote a letter to himself about his reading experiences in eleventh grade, when he managed to read 125 books, some required but most self-selected.

Schizophrenic Ramblings

Dear Rob,

I remember ninth grade, when we had to write about two literary letters to ourselves every quarter. I always thought that was a really silly idea. I thought it might be more fun if we were to respond, as well. However, I get the feeling that teachers are not allowed to inspire schizophrenic behavior among their students. I've always believed that all of us are schizophrenic at some level, even if it's not enough for us to require psychological counseling. We all present different parts of ourselves to different people. However, Mr. Mahoney's idea of a *Backwards Glance* on our literary notebook is one that seems to have a lot of merit. It allows us to evaluate ourselves, and we all know that we are the only ones who can truly judge ourselves.

A Backward Glance
Reflecting on the Writer's Notebook
And Lit. Log
At the end of the quarter

This is not just an opinion.
Give evidence from your notebooks.

Writer's Notebook

- What is your strongest (or most important) entry? Why? What importance does it have for you, the person? For you, the writer?

- What is your weakest entry or one you're least interested in showing or even keeping?

- Where were you when you did most of your writing? Your best writing?

- Are you better off when a topic is given or put on the board or do you write best when you are alone and with your own thoughts and observations?

- What kind of growth or change have you seen in your writer's notebook? How important is this notebook to you?

- If a fire destroyed your things, how upset would you be if your notebook were lost? How useful or tedious has it become to you?

- Did you write anything this quarter because of something you read?

Literary Log

- What is you best lit. letter? How do you know? What do you use to rate it?

- Which letter would you like to show to a college recruiter? To your best friend? Someone else?

- Which letter was your poorest? Why? Is this a pattern?

- What were the best responses you received from others? Why? Did anyone give you good feedback or make a good comment or recommendation to you?

- What was your best reading experience? Why? How did you choose or hear about those books?

- What progress did you make regarding your lit. letters?

FIGURE 3–3. *A Backward Glance: Reflecting on the Writer's Notebook and Lit. Log*

Choosing my best letter from all of the ones I had written this year was no easy task. I read over, or skimmed over, most of them, until I came upon a letter I had written in the last quarter to Elizabeth Farrell. It was my attempt to rectify myself in her eyes, for she had been very disappointed with the last letter I had written her. I was actually trying to see how she would react to another. (Yes, I know, I was playing mind games again.) How do I know it was one of the best? I believe it approaches what I believe a literary letter should be, keeping a dialogue going between Elizabeth and myself, which is the purpose of normal letters. I was simply combining a friendly letter and a literary analysis into one piece. As well, conversation can serve to break up a literary letter. I may enjoy writing letters, and I always love to hear from my friends, but even I know that literary letters can get terribly monotonous to read at times. I rated it as the best piece, in my opinion, because I thought it truly approached the type of letter I would like to see in my portfolio, and I plan on actually using this one as one of the two which I will display within the final portfolio.

The letter I would show to a college recruiter, (if I was going to a college who was deeply concerned with my accomplishments in English), would be a letter I wrote to Mr. Mahoney in the second quarter. It too included a conversation, but I believe its structure was more formal than the letter I had written to Elsabet. Erm, that is, Elizabeth. I was also impressed with Mr. Mahoney's response. The one I would most like to show to my friends? I'm not really sure. There are so many letters which talk about interesting things. I have absolutely no need to impress my friends with my letters, and would like to show them the most interesting of them all. I guess I would show them the same one, the one I had written to Mr. Mahoney. I hit upon many interesting subjects within that letter, including some figures of Fantasy Literature. (These came up in response to something which he had mentioned in his response to my last letter.)

My poorest letter? A measly one pager I wrote to Jeff. One page typed, so it met the requirements of a literary letter, but it hardly approaches the caliber of my better letters. This is the kind of letter I would put in a book with the nice caption: This is how not to write a literary letter. I maintain absolutely no correspondence with my good friend since third grade within the letter, and my analysis of To Kill a Mockingbird is lacking as well. I can only say I may have been pressed for time at the time, or not entirely paying attention to what I was doing.

Now, I say in all seriousness, the best responses I have ever gotten come directly—from my teacher. And I'm not saying this to score bonus points or any such nonsense, for he will most likely never even read this analysis. He is the only person, I believe, who takes the time to read my entire entry, and answers most of the questions that I pose during the course of the letter. As well, he once took the time to type my response onto nice letterhead paper, and gave me stickers as well. Of course, this was the same response which lost some when being printed, but it was nevertheless a great response. He has also recommended books to me that I might consider reading, and he seems to seriously consider recommendations I make of my own to him.

My best reading experience was undoubtedly The Wheel of Time series. The first six books by Robert Jordan were some of the best fantasy literature I had read since J. R. R. Tolkien's books. I chose them simply because they were fantasy literature, and were big books, so they lasted me pretty long. There was another group of books I had found interesting, but I didn't read as many of them, (mainly because others didn't exist), and I cannot remember the author's name at the moment. The books by Jordan were a great experience because he created his fantasy world and the characters within it with a great amount of skill, and I was drawn closely to his books. However, I was disappointed in his seventh book, *Crown of Swords*, I believe it was named, I think it was lacking in the action department.

Progress within my literary letters? I think it was really random. By this time of the year I know what I want to see in a good literary letter, but sometimes I was just too—lazy to write one. I think, however, one can see that my letters are, overall, better written nearer the end of the year, if I had taken the time to make the letter a good one.

This log isn't incredibly important to me . . . but I would be upset if it burned. There are some memories in here, in my correspondence, and it could remind me of books that I read this year as well. I'd miss my stereo system if it burned, but I think this log is more important to me than the books which I wrote my responses about. Within here I have the words of my friends, and the feelings which were in my head when I wrote all the letters, right after reading the books. I'm sure it will land in a box somewhere, but I would not throw this out; there are probably close to 100 pages in the literary log describing how books made me feel. 100 pages typed! I would hate to see so much time going to waste.

Well . . . I've answered all the questions, Rob, so I'll let you go now. Don't write back to yourself; your friends may question your sanity even more than they do now.

Love,
Rob

Adrienne Lu completed her portfolio before I started asking students to write a reflection on their literary logs, but she had some insights into the process that she included in her "Dear Reader" letter:

Dear Reader,

This portfolio represents a year's worth of my writing, along with brief reflections on each piece, in Mr. Mahoney's 11 Honors English class. I have carefully chosen these pieces to be representative of my abilities as a writer. Although writing usually isn't easy for me, it has become a great part of my life.

Thanks to Mr. Newcombe, my A.P. English teacher, for my title. In A.P., Mr. Newcombe constantly tells his students to read books (old as they may be) as if the ink on the pages were still wet. I'd like to think of wet ink as the antithesis of dead, dry ink. Annie Dillard writes in *The Writing Life*, "The written word is weak. Many people prefer life to it. Life gets your blood going, and it smells good. Writing is mere writing, literature is mere. It appeals only to the subtlest senses—the imagination's vision, and the imagination's hearing—and the moral sense, and the moral intellect . . . An ordinary reader picking up a book can't yet hear a thing; it will take half an hour to pick up the writing's modulations, its ups and downs and louds and softs" (17). So my advice, dear reader, is to read as the uncommon reader: take the time to listen, for only then will writing mean anything more than funny symbols on a piece of paper.

As a writer, I feel like a prisoner. Confined within narrow confines (my brain) I must find the best way possible to express myself. Every word becomes precious; excess equals waste. I write, revise, edit, and re-edit. And then I'm done. I may never know who is touched by my writing. I will never know how good or bad it actually is. I write for myself, and when I'm done, my words go out the window (so to speak).

One part of the reading/writing workshop is the writer's notebook, in which we are supposed to jot down anything we might later be able to turn into a piece of writing. At times, I found my writer's notebook to be very helpful; it provided a place for me to keep all my writing ideas which would have otherwise been forgotten. At other times, however, I found myself filling up my writer's notebook with nonsense simply to fulfill the quota. I guess, though, by looking at the number of actual pieces of writing I obtained from my writer's notebook, it was well worth its while.

The second half of the workshop was reading. Although I could not have possibly provided a reflection on all of the books I've read this year (between two English classes!), I have included in this portfolio three literary letters and a reading log (for 11H) for the year. If I were to single out my greatest growth in writing, it would have to be literary letters. Comparing my 11th grade literary letters to my ninth grade letters is evidence of my growth as a reader. Instead of running out of things to write about in a book, I am now running out of room in my literary logs.

Thank you for taking the time to read this letter. Go through my portfolio and read all or none of my writing, as you wish. Just remember one thing, please: the ink is still wet!

Sincerely yours,
Adrienne

Record of Books Read

In the back of their literary logs, students fill out a chart that lists the books they read and, for each book, the date completed, the number of pages, and a rating from 1 to 5. I ask students to include this record in their final portfolio because it helps them look at what they have accomplished and examine the range and depth of their reading for the year. It also helps readers of the portfolio recognize the literary experiences the student has had. I find nothing more astounding at the end of the year than the collections of books read by students. I am thrilled when students move from reading the typical five or six books to reading twenty, thirty, or more. They would probably never have read so many books in a traditional classroom. When working with students, I decided to keep my own list of books read; it now includes all the books I've read in the last thirteen years. This list is something I treasure. Having students include their reading lists in their portfolios creates a record that might be a source of pride to them years from now.

Sheila, an outstanding reader and writer all her life, as well as a member of the volleyball and tennis teams and editor of the literary magazine, included twenty-four books as diverse as *Pilgrim at Tinker Creek* and *All the Pretty Horses*. Bill Reilly, a conscientious student in my regular eighth-grade class who became a fine athlete in high school, showed in his reading list such sophisticated works as *Up Country* and *Roberto Clemente*. Marissa, a student in my regular tenth-grade class, didn't have as many titles as Bill or Sheila did, but her choices nevertheless ranged widely, from very easy to more challenging:

Marissa's List of Books Read

Title	Author	Pages
The Babysitter	R. L. Stine	167
Bury Me Deep	Christopher Pike	211
Clockers	Richard Price	630
The Eyes of Darkness	Dean Koontz	369
Glimmer	Annie Waters	372
Go Ask Alice	Anonymous	327

			The Nitty-Gritty Details	41

Locas   Yxta Maya Murray   458
Lord of the Flies   William Golding   208
To Kill a Mockingbird   Harper Lee   284
25 and Under Fiction   Susan Ketchin & Neil Giordano 563
While My Pretty One Sleeps   Mary Higgins Clark   330
                                            Total   3919

Biographical Poem/Sketch of Writer with Picture

Students are aware that their portfolios may be read by people who don't know them personally, and that these readers might like some behind-the-scenes glimpses of who the writer is. When students look at published books, they find a picture of the author and a brief account of his or her life and accomplishments. Students think some of these accounts are too sketchy—they want more information. Especially when they've heard an author speak on tape or on the radio, they like to see what the person looks like. Sometimes students find that earlier and later works by an author use the same old biography.

Students also read poetry that provides a biographical view. They read Lawrence Ferlinghetti's poem "Autobiography," which begins, "I am leading a quiet life at Mike's Place every day." Then they read a variation of the poem that Richie Weismann wrote for his students as a model, an idea he borrowed from Bill Picchioni, an English teacher in Lynbrook, Long Island. Students look at how the two poems begin and end with the same image, bringing the reader full circle. Here is Richie Weismann's poem:

Autobiography

I have heard the clang of 10,000 lockers
and stalked the tiled hallways past
miles and miles of kaleidoscope classrooms.
Voices drifted out,
speaking in the tongues of a thousand shapers:
Copernicus, Jefferson, Dickens, Pythagorus,
Flaubert, Freud, Shakespeare, Picasso,
J. D. Salinger.
The voices take me back.
I am a boy in Flushing (funny name,
sounds of toilets) where a beech tree weeps
near a Quaker house, while all around
apartment buildings sprout, higher than oak trees.
I rode a Schwinn down the hills of Kissena
where fat carp dined on Wonder Bread.
I liked Ike.
I knew Korea was overrun with red gorillas.
Jersey was summer then.
Country girls with scraped knees ran through my life.

I worried about girls,
my complexion,
wearing glasses,
being tough,
math.
I have been around the world with Bo Diddly,
on Blueberry Hill with Fats,
traded youth for uniform with Elvis.
Shaven-headed,
I have ridden Greyhounds all night
with Semper Fi still echoing through the weekends
on Holden's streets.
I went on the road with Kerouac.
I stared doom in the eye on an October day
as Jack and Kiki played chicken in Fidel's yard.
I ordered lunch—hot pastrami—while Jackie screamed
in the back seat of a limo
in Dallas.
I heard the bullets keep ringing out
and smelled the stench of war wafting
through news print
and air waves
while skinny girls blew soap bubbles at
Woodstock.
I was glad to welcome a long sea wave
to the churning pebbled shore of Montauk
where I once shared a boulder with a swashbuckling tern.
I tip-toed past Watergate, the Ayatollah,
gas lines, leisure suits, Reagonomics,
bull markets, baby boomers, and gray hair.
But the clang of the lockers
and the drone of voices
still call cadence for my march.

In the spirit of this poem, I ask students to write a brief sketch of their life and to include a representative picture, perhaps one from the yearbook or a recent portrait. The sketch can be in any form they want, prose or poetry, but it should provide information for the reader. Then I ask the students to try doing a biographical sketch in their writer's notebook. It is not a requirement that they end the final portfolio with a sketch, but some like the sketches they have produced and want to use them in the portfolio. Chance are, almost no one would include a sketch if I didn't ask them to try it, if I just showed them the poems as a possibility and then moved on.

Sheila Erimez used this biographical sketch format for her poem "A Few of My Favorite Things." Instead of using just one picture, she placed six color pictures of her favorite places and activities to the right of the poem on a two-page layout. She placed a graphic that looks like the edge of 16 mm film running down both sides of the pictures, creating the illusion that her life was running—like a film—before our very eyes.

A Few of My Favorite Things

I am living in a white-walled house
down by the beach,
thoroughly enjoying
the simple things in life.
I am a girl who is fascinated by nature.
I have always been a girl who is fascinated by nature.
I have laughed with joy
as a hungry-eyed seagull
snatched a French fry from my hand.
I have swam through crystal blue waters
in the sun-kissed islands of Gocek
I have stood on the shore of the magnificent Bosporus,
and looked across
to see a whole other continent entirely—Asia.
I have stared in silent awe, open-mouthed in my doorway
at the beautiful black grand piano
placed in my livingroom as a surprise gift to me.
I have felt the joy
of being the first to cross the line
in the 55 meter dash.
I have felt the air shatter around me
as I sat in a New York City window sill,
watching the brilliant, thundering fireworks
that flew from the barges on the Hudson River.
I have seen bizarre works of art
at the Biennial art show in the Whitney Museum—
dirty mattresses bound together, smeared with cake,
and hung from the ceiling . . .
a hearse split in half,
covered with a thick layer of grease,
and placed in a cage atop old, rusting mufflers.
Strange—but they got you thinking.
I have read *Romeo and Juliet*,
and loved every page of it.
I have felt the anxiety
of walking into the judging room at NYSSMA,
where I was to play the tattered, mahogany piano,
as well as the uplifting pride
of receiving a perfect score.
I have sported a smile all day
when I found out my poem had won first place

in the Eastern Suffolk Writing Contest.
I have smelled the burning
of a bonfire on the beach at night,
mixing with the salty air,
as I sat nearby on the cool sand
surrounded by friends and fellow classmates.
I have passed many summer hours
happily swimming and tanning on that beach,
or watching the sky grow warm
with golden sunset hues.
I have sailed across the Sound
to Block Island,
where I galloped on horseback
down along the oceanside
with the wind in my face,
taking in the mystical view.
I am the girl
in the white-walled house
down by the beach, and forever will I enjoy
the simple things in life.

Other students wrote traditional prose accounts of themselves. Jody Shenn wrote his biographical sketch in third person, creating a certain distance for himself as he presented the accomplishments of his life:

Born on October 3, 1977 to parents Frederic and Patrice, Joseph Benjamin Shenn picked up a nickname on his way out of the birth canal, and has been called Jody ever since. It was on his first pieces of writing that this pen name was immediately challenged—his kindergarten teachers required poor Jody to memorize all six letters of his more proper name. The fact that he was reading well before any schooling—by the early age of two—mattered not to Mrs. Krauza, who just couldn't accept J-O-D-Y as sufficient education. This may be part of the learning block Jody still has today against both spelling and remembering people's names.

Jody has grown up in a reading/writing environment, being read to many nights as a youngster out of such advanced books as *The Never-Ending Story* and *The Yearling*. He surprised his parents by reading the lines ahead of them out of his favorite book, *Hop on Pop* by Doctor Seuss. That was age two; it was partly understanding the letters, but mostly remembering the dozens of times it was read to him before. It contained the word "Timbuktu" which is an accomplishment any toddler can be proud of. Later, during his early adolescence, his Grandmother greatly encouraged his reading by bringing along presents of literature. Grandma brought him 12 books of the Oz series by Frank Baum, and more than 20 Hardy

Boys mysteries. She always complained of not knowing what books to bring him, but he devoured them no matter what they were.

Mr. Shenn is no best selling author, and hasn't written any screenplays as of yet. But he does take great pleasure in " . . . writing something good. Something I could give to someone just because I'm proud of it. I want my writing to be loved, maybe more than I want to be loved. That is probably why I put everything I have into it."

His past portfolios include: *Excuse Me While I Kiss the Sky*—a collection of his 1993, 10th grade English work. It was mostly overlooked by the commercial world, but is a cult gem. At least to him, it is. He is currently working on his first short book *It's the End of the World and Even the Roaches are Dead* and is planning to make it good enough to be proud of. As of now, though, his major chunk of attention is focused on doing whatever necessary to get into the top colleges. Jody Shenn lives in Miller Place, NY.

Cover

At first I required portfolio front covers to have the information that is typically on essays: name, date, teacher, grade level, period, etc. In time, I gave the cover design back to the students. Authors often include only their title and their own name. They may include an illustration, some words from a poem or a song, or some other artistic touches. I've come to realize that the cover should somehow depict the theme of the portfolio and connect the theme to the title. Other information is found on the inside, on the title page. Students and I looked at published books to see what information they give inside. We found places of publication, copyright information, and Library of Congress numbers. In keeping with the idea of producing a book, some students make up their own publishing houses and list warnings about copyright infringement penalties.

Rob Wahl began his portfolio with a series of sentences to make it look like a published book:

Two Worlds Meet:
The Clash of Ego and Spirit

1997 Copyright ROB, Inc.
All Rights Reserved

NOTE: If you are viewing this portfolio without a cover, you should be aware that this portfolio is stolen property. It was reported as "unsold and destroyed" to the publisher, and neither the author nor the publisher has received any payment for this "stripped portfolio."

This portfolio is protected under the copyright laws of the United States of America. Any reproduction or other unauthorized use of the material contained herein is prohibited without the express written permission of ROB, Inc.

First Printing: June 1997
Printed in the United States of America
Library of Congress Catalog Card Number: 95-92303
098765432
ISBN: 0-7907-7907-9

ROB, Inc.
Miller Place, NY 11764-1905
U. S. A.

ROB, Inc. is a fictional corporation created for the sole purpose of
lending a sense of validity to this page. Please take note of the dis-
claimer/copyright pages connected to: "Bishop Senshi Sailor Moon
Meets <u>The Wheel of Time</u>" and "The Diabolical Idiot: Who?"

When students begin to take their publications seriously, they want the
authentic look of a real book, even if they have to fool around a little and
create fictitious companies and book registration numbers.

Other Portfolio Contents

Over the years, I have experimented with other things that might go in the
final portfolio. For example, one year I wondered if students' interest in their
portfolios would carry into the summer, so I asked them to make a list of
books they might like to read over the summer. Most wanted to continue
reading, thinking that the ten weeks of summer would be a time of complete
freedom and idyllic reading. In reality, summer sports teams, camps, jobs,
friends, and the beach on the Long Island Sound were allurements that the
average teenager just couldn't resist. Of course, some continued their reading,
but at a much reduced rate. The goal of students' doing summer reading was
more a wish on my part than reality. The idea of actual summer reading assignments is another issue. Suffice it to say that I have found that assigning
summer reading often does more harm than good.

Reader Responses

Each portfolio includes a sheet at the end on which readers can write their
responses to the student's work. Some students provide several blank pages
with "Comments, Please" typed at the top. Others go further to persuade
readers to write a response. One of the more personal requests for responses
was Jody Shenn's final comment, in which he passes the theme of his portfolio, *I Ching, The Book of Change*, along to his readers:

All right, Reader. You've read the portfolio. You've been changed (This is the *I Ching*, after all). Now, how about you do some work in making this the best portfolio ever! (GO, NEW YORK! Goooo!) I want you to get out there and write some comments on what you've seen and what you've read. Go ahead—no need to be afraid. I would have attached a pen with one of those little chains for you but I was worried you'd steal it anyway. So, take a second out of your life to fill it with what your take is on what I've tried to do, and how well I've accomplished it. Don't pull any punches with me. I can take a little honest criticism. (Very little.) I poured many hours into this and I'd love to hear something about it from an unprejudiced pen. Go ahead, I think you're ready . . .

Some students print an invitation at the top of a piece of paper, asking for readers to respond with at least a signature, as in a guest book, or with a brief comment. Sometimes the person to whom a portfolio is dedicated, or another of the student's significant others, is so moved by the work that they want to write back. At our inservice workshops, Jerry and I ask teachers to write substantial responses to the student portfolios they read, describing the time and place they're reading in. These teachers might have just flown into an NCTE (National Council of Teachers of English) convention the night before. They might have raced through the downpour of an Orlando cloudburst or braced themselves against Chicago sleet, or they might be lolling around a pool in San Diego. This information creates a live context by giving students a sense of the state of mind of the teachers who are responding to their portfolios. Reading these responses can be illuminating and inspiring for students, adding icing on the cake of their spectacular creations.

What follows is a sampling of the scores of letters teachers have written in response to the student portfolios they've read. The first is from a student teacher who was in a seminar I taught.

Dear Sheila,

I have just now finished a brief viewing of your portfolio and wish I had more time to spend with it—and you. I am a graduate student at Stony Brook in a seminar with Mr. Mahoney. At present, I am student teaching at Kings Park Middle School. I wish I could drag you, and your portfolio, to school with me tomorrow morning. I wish I could take you home with me tonight and pore over the pages of poetry and prose.

You are a wonderful writer. You are a sailor . . . me too! I know that look in your eyes as you spread your body over the main sail. I love the images you create with words and the depth of your young (and surprisingly experienced) mind! "Creation" reminded me of Whitman's "Song of Myself." Well, it's been a brief space in time I

have spent with you here on this page that does your portfolio such
little justice. Thank you for sharing!

Ruth O'Shea

The teachers at the conferences we do our workshops at have come to
learn from the sessions they attend, and they have a sense of anticipation
and appreciation. Many write letters like Elizabeth's:

Dear Jody—

*Wow! I teach 9th and 11th grade Hawaiian students at the Kamehe-
meha Schools in Honolulu, HI. I would like to take your portfolio home
with me to help inspire my students. It shows much work, thought, reflection, and love. Your "Two Poems of Two" and the remarks about
them really moved me. (I passed them to my neighbor to read and to
enjoy also!) I don't have nearly enough time to do this beautiful portfolio justice by close and savoring reading.*
  In fact, I wish I could kidnap you to come and inspire my students!
  *Keep reading. (I love A Prayer for Owen Meany!) Keep writing! Keep
living!*

A hui hon. Malama pono.
(Farewell. Take good care.)
Elizabeth French Truesdell

Sometimes a portfolio brings the reader to tears. Sister Nora explains
that to Erin:

Dear Erin,

I was really touched by your portfolio. You have great insights and
I admire the fact that your would rewrite a piece from two years
ago when you were in ninth grade and realize that you have grown
emotionally and in your perceptions.
  Erin, I cried when I read your poem, "Remembering Mom."
Maybe I cried for your pain, but I also cried for my own, because
my Mom died 12 years ago yesterday, and I still feel the pain of loss.
  Continue to express your feelings through what you write,
Erin, and "Never Shame to Hear What You Have Nobly Done."
(Shakespeare)

Love,
Sr. Nora
Holy Trinity HS
Hicksville, NY

Sometimes teachers borrow some of the portfolios to use in their own
classrooms as models so their students can study them at length. Here is a

Kerri—

I was so impressed with your portfolio. In fact, I used it as a model for my 8th grade classes during the '98–99 school year. They too loved your work and made an attempt to create portfolios that were similar to this one.

My two favorite pieces are "Wasted Dreams" and "Twisted Tale"—both really touched me. They send a message to all of us. We seem to share a bad quality—we both write our best late at night, last minute. You have a special gift. Best of luck in all of your future endeavors.

Sincerely,
Mrs. Michele Sullivan
Oregon Middle School

Sometimes a portfolio touches home and resonates with a student's parent. Lauren Fasullo's parents, both teachers, had divorced shortly before her eighth-grade year, when she created *The Division Bell*, a title derived from a Pink Floyd album. In the portfolio is a prose piece she wrote:

The Division Bell

Separation among others is mutual. Dragged by the force of some inner tide. Once you have seen the separation occur, you will no longer face life with the same view that you have always looked at it before. It puts a gap in your heart, and it's a loss that you cannot face without hurt. Wishing the division would stop only makes the hurt more painful. Stuck in a world of isolation, while the ivy grows over the doors, you wait. Wait for the moment in time where the ringing stops abruptly.

Now life devalues day by day, for the ringing of the division bell has had its way. Leaves you breathlessly behind as you run the next race. If you do not win it, you must try again. Cautiously as you take each step, your mind tries to put the sound of the continuous ringing elsewhere.

Knowing you can do nothing but suffer, you give up. Give up your chance of ever having the ringing end. Now you have no choice but to go on with life, even though there will always be a Division Bell in your way.

Lauren's reflection on the piece read as follows:

You may think this is a very confusing piece but if you really think about it, you will probably understand it. This piece refers to my life. It is divided because of my parents' divorce. I feel as if I am divided into two lives and I can't do anything about it. When I refer to the bell ringing in this piece, I am referring to my parents' divorce. It is not an easy situation for others that are involved. When others read this piece, they feel confused. They should try to read it fully and try to compare it to my life and see if they know what it is about. This was included in my portfolio obviously because the title is the theme of my portfolio.

Lauren's mom read the portfolio that summer and wrote this response:

> "And a woman said, speak to us of children. And he said: Your children are not your children. They are the sons and daughters of life's longing for itself. They come through you yet they do not belong to you. You may give them your love but not your thoughts, for they have their own thoughts. You may strive to be like them, but seek not to make them like you. For life goes not backward nor tarries with yesterday . . ."
>
> —from *The Prophet* by Kahil Gibran

Dear Lauren,

This is from one of my favorite books and I wanted to share it with my daughter, the writer (a very well kept secret this year!) *The Division Bell* has enabled me, through tears, to feel what you have been feeling. As I used to do as a teenager, you have used the medium of poetry to express your pain, your frustration with life. It is a wonderful way to share with others, a very important outlet. I hope that you continue to grow in your writing and reach your goals, whatever they may be. Always know that I love you and will be there for you at every turn . . .

Mom

In September, Lauren's dad had a chance to read her portfolio and to write a response.

Dear Lauren,

Wow! What a beautiful collection of writings.

Just knowing that you picked Pink Floyd as your theme made the readings even more special for me. Remember the day we sat at the piano and played the notes to "High Hopes" together?

Sadly, The Division Bell had become a reality in both our lives. You have expressed yourself so genuinely and maturely. You have a true talent for expressive writing. Please continue to use this gift to help you through the many difficulties that surely lie ahead.

I am so very proud of you and your accomplishments. I love you with everything that is me.

Daddy

My own responses to students' portfolios have been both long and short. Some have been written in haste as a school year comes to an end; others, in leisure during the summer. I have written straightforward prose reactions. At other times, I have written poems as a way of revealing what I experienced reading the student's work. Some portfolios have sent me looking for poems by published authors that express the ideas or themes that the student has written about.

There is no grade, state test, or final examination that can measure the impact of writing on students and on those who read their work. Some of the teachers who read student portfolios in Jerry's and my workshops find inspiration to enrich the lives of their own students in a new way. Other readers get a glimpse into a teenager's soul and realize that young and old have much in common. Still other readers, such as parents, find a chance to see a child through a different lens and to cry at the view.

4 | A WRITING STATE OF MIND

What teachers should worry about . . . what I am most concerned with—is our students' linguistic confidence. I want students to develop a willingness to be bold with language, to press forward with words. I want them to be versatile, daring, and practiced enough to interact readily with their writing and to do so with imagination, logic, and originality.

Tom Romano,
Writing with Passion

For writing to abound, students need to be in a constant writing state of mind, writing mentally even when they aren't writing physically. They must be so used to writing that they are always rehearsing writing, thinking about writing a piece before actually beginning to write, as Tom Romano suggests (1995). Ideas for writing may be on the front burner, ready to be put down on paper, or they may be just about to be recognized by a writer who has found in the everyday events of life possible subjects for a piece of writing.

I try to be in a writing state of mind. One morning as I was leaving the community college, I looked down the hill into a student parking lot before getting into my car. I saw a black Honda hatchback, beeping loudly, that seemed to be bearing down on a girl who was on her way to class, causing her to scream out in fright and turn toward the car. Just then, she recognized her girlfriend behind the wheel and began cursing and laughing at her friend for frightening her. Although the friend seemed to accept this as normal behavior, I thought it was a bad joke, that the driver was cruel to scare her friend.

As the girl continued to class, the driver opened her window a little and dropped out a big ball of paper, letting it fall to the ground in the middle of the parking lot. This littering seemed to me clearly intentional and I wanted to run down the hill and yell at the driver to pick up the paper. A few minutes later, I noticed a girl who looked like the litterbug walking up the path. I hesitated, finding myself partly ashamed for not speaking up, partly angry at this girl's joke and her indifferent littering. I also found myself planning how to write about it. I thought about a poem that I might show to my students, a letter to the college newspaper, even an epistle to the driver, who I'd track down through her license plate. I went home and wrote the events in my writer's notebook, planning to create a poem about careless human beings, like Gatsby's Daisy and other carelessly cruel people of that rich, arrogant world.

My wondering about how I might write about this experience is an example of being in a writing state of mind. I felt a need, because I'd been working with student writers, to make the story into a statement about my beliefs. I was preparing to write even when I wasn't writing. Being in a writing state of mind is a habit. It can be cultivated by using various approaches that can be taught in a writing classroom. Earlier that same morning, with only four weeks to go in the semester, I asked students to list their reflections on their accomplishments, skills learned, attitudes acquired, and ideas more fully understood or adopted. Darren said that he had learned he could write notes about an incident and go back to them later and still find them fresh enough to develop into a whole piece of writing. Mike added that he had learned to bring his writer's notebook with him everywhere, including to his workplace, and to trust that when he made some quick notes he would later be able to develop them into something fuller.

Being in a writing state of mind comes from being in an environment that allows for writing every day or every class period. When students can count on being able to write as they count on the sun coming up, they can come to class knowing they will have time to work on their writing—perhaps starting a fresh piece that germinated as an idea jotted down outside of class in the writer's notebook. For example, Marissa Hahn was sitting in her room when the words from a Toni Braxton song, "Secrets," developed into connected thoughts for her. Because Marissa was in a writing state of mind, she picked up her writer's notebook and started writing furiously. Marissa learned, as Tom Romano says, to "trust the gush" that comes in such moments. She created lines with an *abcb* rhyme scheme when she remembered to craft her words and ideas into a meaningful, skilled format. The final form that she produced was pleasing to her, so much so that she placed it at the beginning of her portfolio.

The Cheater's Lies

I felt something wrong as I walked into your hell.
I entered your house without ringing your bell.
The tenseness engulfed my body as I strolled into your room.
Hesitating the moment as I smelled her perfume.
You leaped up, my presence an immense surprise.
Losing the grasp of her, I was the intensity in your eyes.
I wanted to disappear, I wished it wasn't real.
Feeling the pain and confusion swell no longer could I feel.
It was all a game we were playing as I ran back to you.
Your arms enclosed around me.
I knew it was too good to be true.
And as I stood there, numb from head to toe,
I realized your love was fake but I was too blind to know.
No longer can I take in the pain and anguish you've given my
    heart.
My life shattering into nothing, I retreat to the start.
I leave your room, never looking into your eyes.
I achieved my heart and mind and left behind all your lies.

Reflection on "The Cheater's Lies"

This is a very emotional poem. It describes a girl walking in on her boyfriend cheating on her. This particular piece of writing has much meaning to me. In my mind, cheating is the worst thing you could do in a relationship. I feel that if you need to be with someone else, you shouldn't have a boyfriend/girlfriend in the first place. It makes me so aggravated to think that someone could cheat on a person—nobody deserves that much pain.

One day, I was listening to my Toni Braxton CD. There was a song on there, "Secrets," that just put these thoughts and feelings into my mind. I sat down and started writing. I wanted to create a setting—she walks into a room, maybe an apartment they are sharing. She knew something was wrong, she sensed it:

> The tenseness engulfed my body as I strolled into your
>   room.
> Hesitating the moment as I smelled her perfume.

I can remember watching movies and hearing stories from friends that reminded me of these sentences. They would say that they thought their boyfriend was cheating on them, they could smell it. I put myself in their shoes and tried to see how I would feel. . . .

THE WRITER'S NOTEBOOK

At the heart of the writing "program" is the writer's notebook. In the late 1970s and through the 1980s, my students kept journals, marble-covered composition notebooks in which they wrote on topics of their choice, including incidents that happened to them and the thoughts that were on their minds. Seniors used the notebooks to work through on paper the decisions they were facing about having to select a college. Many would sit down to write with no idea which college they really wanted to attend (and would say so), but by the end of their journal deliberations, they would have made a clear and certain decision. They were using the journal to figure out their lives for themselves.

Typically, I would assign ten journal entries for a ten-week quarter. I'd take the journals home, read them, and comment on a few entries, basically shutting myself up for the weekend for this ritual. Despite knowing that many of the entries were done in a frenzy near the end of the marking period, I continued to require journals because I felt that students gained from the exercise. And I would suffer and sacrifice my time, as all "good" teachers and parents do, if it would benefit the kids. Most of my colleagues were doing the same. The process varied slightly, but all seemed overwhelmed by having to read journal entries in addition to grading assigned essays. Then studies in *The English Journal* reported that while journal keeping helped writing fluency to some extent, student writing did not improve enough to warrant all the effort that went into journal keeping. What was I doing? Why was I inflicting such pain on myself and on my students if it didn't make my students better writers? I never connected students' usual assigned writing with their journal writing. I didn't correct the journals or have students revise their entries or develop them into pieces that would be graded.

This is not to say that there weren't many students who enjoyed writing at least some of their journal entries—or that I didn't find joy in reading some of them. Some students embraced the journal as a place to think, and I loved being able to have students talk to me in this way. But eventually I began to move away from reading everything that students wrote. Instead, I asked them to write on a slip of paper included in their journals which two or three entries of the ten I should read. What I didn't realize at the time was that I was asking students to reflect about which entries were more or less interesting, which were more or less valuable.

"No Journals This Year"

When Jerry and I began using the writing/reading workshop in 1989, we never mentioned keeping journals and no students brought it up. Instead, students wrote drafts that they kept in their loose-leaf binders, and they kept a list of "Topics I Can Write About," a record of ideas for future pieces. On December 1, 1989, when we heard Donald Graves speak at Dowling College on Long Island, Jerry and I discovered what was missing from our workshop approach: the writer's notebook. Graves gave the audience of teachers a challenge to "write for ten minutes a day, that's all, no rewrite, just ten minutes." That afternoon, I stopped at a store and bought myself a college-ruled hundred-page spiral notebook. The next day I wrote for almost twenty-four minutes about an incident that had occurred at the end of our presentation the previous day, trying to write in my notebook the way Graves wrote in his:

12/2/89

The woman wearing white in the last row over near the wall raised her hand nervously as the workshop began to break up and the participants closed their notebooks, looked for their handbags, gathered their books, shopping bags, and coats, and made ready to stand up. She was leaning forward, craning her neck, eager to have her say. "This man is right. I just have to say this. Every word he says is true. My son, Raymond Markoff, is in his class and it's true; it's all true!"

Some heads turned to listen, to eye this excited speaker who seemed emotionally moved, who seemed like one wanting something of the crowd and fearful that the crowd would pay no heed. "Oh," said the presenter up front to whom these remarks were directed, "Oh, this is the mother of the boy with the twenty books

---

read so far this year, the one up on the transparency," and he pointed to his left to the overhead projector.

"No," she said, more clearly. "That was Michael Schnaars. My son is Raymond Markoff, Mike's good friend." At that, the presenter opened his mouth in apology and embarrassment for momentarily confusing two of his students.

"My son is in Mr. Mahoney's 11 Honors class," she went on, starting to grow more intense, "and what he's saying really works. It really does. My son is very bright but he never used to read. My husband and I didn't know what's happening." Her eyes, even behind her glasses, seemed more intense. "My husband has the highest praise for you," she said, turning back to the presenter, exhorting the crowd to listen, to take heed, as if the presenter's words were the basis for salvation. It was not as though she were acting foolishly or zealously, or improperly. "Let me tell you it works! We came home at night and the TV wasn't on and he was reading in his room. Mr. Matovcik and Mr. Mahoney, you two should write a book."

She was quite sincere and quite intense. When she finished and sat back down, the presenters ended the workshop by passing out the bookmarks they had made for the participants and announcing the availability of handouts. The workshop formally came to an end . . . and the floodgates opened for the wave of enthusiastic response.

Living Wide-Awake Lives

After I started keeping a writer's notebook and reading excerpts to my students from time to time, I decided to ask them to keep one the following school year. I was further convinced when a few students complained near the end of the year that they were running out of topics to write about. In the beginning of the year we had made long lists of things we could write about in the future. Some ideas panned out, some became merged into a single piece, and some proved not to be fruitful. But now the students seemed stuck and were almost asking me to assign topics. I remembered hearing Lucy Calkins at a NCTE conference tell about flying with her two small sons. The three of them would be alert travelers, noticing everything. She said that they were leading "wide-awake lives" as they paid attention to cloud formations, the terrain below, and even what was happening in the cabin of the plane. Calkins said that they were "paying attention to the lived moments of their lives." She said that students need to have this kind of awareness as they write in their writer's notebooks. They need to record these lived moments in precise detail. Later on, by themselves or with the help of the teacher, they can begin to notice patterns in their recordings. They will begin to see what is "really important to them," though they might not be aware of it when they're writing. By reviewing the pages of their writer's notebooks, students would begin to see topics to write about for their developed, or "finished," pieces. The notebooks would become a tool for collecting infor-

mation the way most writers do and for revisiting it to discover developed
topics that might become "published" pieces.

My notebook is a place where I write from time to time about things that are important to me. I always have it in class so that I can write in it when I ask students to try something in theirs. I allow my students to choose just about any type of notebook that they want: wide-lined or college-ruled, marble-covered or wire-bound, big or small. They select the notebook that works best for them, makes them most comfortable writing in, and has the right paper texture and physical appearance. I encourage them to decorate their writer's notebooks any way they choose. I show them mine, which is covered with Con-Tact paper and has the title *Birch Seedlings and Birch Trimmings—A Writer's Notebook* printed on fancy paper and taped on the front. My name is printed in bold letters, with "May 1995," the date when I began my second writer's notebook. My first is dated December 1989, the date when Donald Graves first challenged us to begin writing for ten minutes a day. On the cover of my first writer's notebook and on every notebook since, I've written "The Ten-Minute-a-Day Challenge from Donald Graves." My writer's notebook is always with me.

Blank Looks

When I first introduced the writer's notebook, I got some blank looks from students who didn't know what to write. Many at first saw the notebooks as a place to write neatly and in a polished format, thinking that they'd later transfer the work to neatly written composition paper pages or type it into the computer. They also saw the notebooks as something that they would hand in for me to read and grade. They didn't yet see the writer's notebooks as theirs, a view that would take some time to develop. So I began with Lucy Calkins' concept of recording the sights, sounds, smells, and other sense details around us. This began in the first day or two of the school year. I'd ask students to write down what they were noticing at that very moment: sounds in the hallway; the weather; how the floor and ceiling looked—dirty or clean, crumbling or smooth. I asked them to notice the other students in the classroom. How many students were wearing sneakers, shoes, or boots? How many students were left-handed? Right-handed? How many wore glasses, rings, watches, or other jewelry? How did students write—bent over, slumped, stopping and starting, furious and vigorously, slowly and deliberately?

For the next five minutes, we all wrote, recording the chirping of a cricket in the corner of the room, the sounds of a tractor outside cutting the grass, the clicking of the clock up on the wall, the wafting of hot air in those dreaded heat waves of early September. In all my classes, the students seemed to be able to record their impressions for long periods of time. Then I would ask them to write what they were thinking, what was on their minds, what they were anticipating later that day. They could even connect these feelings with other things that were going on around them. In some classes, I changed the scene: We'd go outside for a ten-minute walk across the soccer field to the edge of the woods. Sometimes we would slip through the fence and walk the beaten path in the woods on the other side. Always, we stopped periodically to record the sense details. We were generally quiet, but sometimes we pointed out a spider's web among leaves beneath some brush, or a fallen birch tree a few feet off the path. It was amazing to see an entire class of students writing what they saw and heard. We even stopped on our return and looked at the school building from a distance, seeing it as perhaps we'd never seen it before, with time, stillness, and a writer's eye.

When we got back to the classroom, we either continued writing or compared notes. Some students would already be starting to draft a poem or a prose piece about the setting. I asked students to carry their notebooks to other places and to record what was going on around them. They might record a few minutes during study hall in the noisy cafeteria, the scene in a classroom as students got settled and the teacher took attendance, or a conversation they overheard by a locker in the hallway or at another table in the cafeteria. These "lived moments" of the students' lives were worth recording not just for their own sake, but because they helped the students develop a writer's eye for detail. They were doing what Ralph Fletcher suggests in *A Writer's Notebook* (1996): "writing small." I included that and other techniques on "A Writer's Notebook," a handout that summarizes some of the ways of using a writer's notebook that Fletcher recommends (Figure 4–1).

Months later, I read with awe Alan Lemley's account of his writer's notebook experience, which he reflected on in his portfolio.

Memories of My Writer's Notebook

While I can't say that I will continue my writer's notebook after this year is over, I did find that it transformed from a strained requirement in the beginning of the year to a fluid stream of thoughts by the end of the year. My writer's notebook served a variety of purposes that I had not anticipated. When considering what to write, I often found myself reflecting on current events. Although not a diary, my notebook often held the thoughts and stories that seemed important at the time. Upon leafing through my notebook to write this piece of writing, I discovered the following (which appears exactly as it does in my notebook):

> I strode silently to the ship's bow, the soft throbbing of the diesel engines vibrating beneath my feet. It was a serene evening, and the wind whispered gently in my ears, creating a peaceful and almost lulling effect.
>
> Barely making it back in time for the ferry from Bridgeport, Connecticut, my parents and I had arrived no less than one minute before our reservations were forfeited. Leaving my mom reading in the car, Dad and I climbed into the night to stand on the vacant bow of the ferry.

A Writer's Notebook

"A writer's notebook gives you a place to live like a writer," says Ralph Fletcher. A Writer's Notebook is like a compost pile into which ideas are tossed to cook for a time until they are turned over enough to produce rich soil for a new piece of writing. A Writer's Notebook is a place to exercise writing, "a place to stretch or jog around the block!" In Ralph Fletcher's *A Writer's Notebook: Unlocking the Writer Within You*, he hits upon these ideas:

What could go into your Writer's Notebook?

1. Unforgettable Stories: Stories that you read in the newspapers or see on TV. Stories that inspire or tug at the heart strings.
2. Fierce Wonderings: What questions haunt or nag at you, make you wonder?
3. "Write Small": Notice the small details that say so much about a person.
4. Seed Ideas: Ideas that grow into stories after a while.
5. Mind Pictures: Pay attention to your world; write it down; go back and write more.
6. Snatches of Talk: Listen for lines around you.
7. Lists: Things That Irritate Me, Goals, Family Stories, Unusual Words, Favorite Lines from Songs, Favorite Quotations.
8. Memories: Photos, collages, newspaper clippings, drawings, etc.
9. Writing Strikes!: Collect your favorite lines/sentences/words from the authors you read.

FIGURE 4–1. *A Writer's Notebook*

We discussed our hectic trip to visit my brother at Dartmouth. Although there wasn't a soul around, the surroundings seemed to suggest that we talk in hushed tones, for any extraneous noise would be swallowed by the night.

As the ship pointed off into the black unknown, I couldn't help but wonder where our family would be in several years. Would I continue in my brother's footsteps to Dartmouth, as he encouraged me to do so often? What would Erick be doing? Perhaps he would be happily married and finished medical school? Would my mom use her brilliance to find a job? Would my dad be retired or still working on complex issues at Brookhaven National Lab? Perhaps someday I would fully understand the scientific things Dad would so often lecture me about.

My mind remained on these and other thoughts as I perused the fall sky powdered with stars. Upon looking off the starboard bow, I witnessed something I had never before seen in my life. Being on a flat expanse at the right time, I watched as a crescent harvest moon slipped slowly past the watery horizon, leaving a brilliant orange trail across the Long Island Sound. Then the glimmering reflections ceased.

At the onset of the school year, I wasn't sure how to go about using the writer's notebook. Because I knew it was supposed to be the springboard for finished pieces of writing, my first entries were exactly as if I had taken out a piece of paper under forced conditions to write. Mr. Mahoney helped to inspire the random nature of the writer's notebook by asking us to take it out in class and describe something in the room. I found these entries in my notebook about two of my classmates:

> Taras tries to withhold a smile, but he appears to try too hard. The corners of his lips gradually descend and before he knows it, the small fly resting on the ceiling stares through its compound eyes, and sees Taras grinning.

> Colin has made up his mind. As if he had just shoved aside an offensive lineman and has a clear run to sack the quarterback, he picks up his pen and determinably begins to scribble. His large body towers over his paper and he shakes the small object in front of him, finishing with an exclamation mark. Leaving his fallen foe on the ground, he returns to the huddle for a new plan.

As the year progressed, my writing became a more fluid extension of my thoughts. My stories ranged further into my past and became less of a task to write. I noticed that my writing contained fewer mistakes and often ran from one page to the next as I became absorbed in my writing. Towards the end of the year, my writer's notebook entries reached the point where I could virtually pick a story and type it up to be handed in without making a single correction. My writer's notebook had become a valuable possession.

The Compost Heap

Unlike Alan, not all students found that their writing toward the end of the year was virtually the same as what was in their writer's notebooks. Most still saw the notebooks as the place to collect things for later use. The writer's notebook is a compost heap, as Lucy Calkins calls it, on which we throw the organic scraps from our everyday lives: egg shells, vegetable peelings, coffee grounds, even grass clippings and leaves. We just let the stuff pile up, one layer on top of another. Periodically, we go out and turn it over, giving air to the material, which is in the stage of transformation. In time, we find that the heap contains very rich soil for growing new things. As we record the lived moments of our lives in a writer's notebook, we let entries pile up for a while. Every so often we return to the notebook and turn over the pages, giving a little air and light to the entries, perhaps seeing material that is ready for use in a piece of writing.

At the end of each marking period, I ask students to look back at their writer's notebook entries for the previous ten weeks, then to use the hand-out "A Backward Glance" (Figure 3–3) to write a reflection in the notebook about their discoveries for that quarter. Having students reflect frequently allows them to see their progress more clearly. It also allows them to write a thorough reflection on how they use the writer's notebook that they can include in the final portfolio.

Quick Writes

One way to add material to the writer's notebook is to give students regular opportunities to do daily *quick writes*, quickly fashioned responses that complete a prompt. When I say, "Okay, writer's notebooks out for some quick writes," students open to the next available spot in their notebooks, put the date at the top, and listen for the prompt. I usually have the prompts at least partially written on the board, then I fill in the rest. We do three quick writes, one minute each. The prompts can be anything that allows students to write almost immediately about some aspect of their lives.

For eighth graders, I ask them to copy down the prompt "When I was a beginning seventh grader, I. . . ." I tell them they have one minute to write as fast as they can about whatever comes to mind, then set my watch and say "go." Sometimes I write as they write, while at other times I observe the way different students compose, looking for potential trouble spots. As the time ticks down, I act like a coach running his team through wind sprints, encouraging them to finish hard, asking them to "dig it out," urging them to grab "just one more image" in the remaining ten seconds.

After one minute, I give a second prompt, such as "I'll never forget that glorious day when. . . ." Before I start the students this time, I remind them that the prompt is only a suggestion. If they want to change the first prompt from "seventh grade" to "sixth grade," that's fine. If they wanted to change "glorious" in the second prompt to "horrible," that's their choice. If they are writing rapidly and an unrelated idea suddenly pops into their minds, they should "go with the surprise," as Donald Murray suggested (1992). Murray said that we write to be surprised, to learn what we aren't thinking—to discover. If students find a surprise in the images they are recording, they can abandon the previous thoughts at least for a while and explore the new ones. The purpose of this activity is to get ideas onto the page so they can be turned into something later on. Before I start students on the second prompt, I warn them to lower their standards, advice from the poet William Stafford. He would say, "We're not interested in your writing good stuff," just in getting the ideas out as accurately as possible. So I say, "Lower your standards and race that pen across the page. No idea should be rejected as stupid or dumb. Don't sit being a critic. Just get it out. Ready—go!"

I have little concern for the actual seconds on the clock. I let the least fluent student in the class tell me when it is time to stop. If I see heads come up after thirty-five seconds, I give the students another five seconds and then stop them. I don't want this writing to be a drag, nor do I want any weak students to distract other students. After the first quick write, I often ask the students to count the number of lines they've written and tell them that the average student writes about five lines in one minute. Some have more while some have less, depending on the size of their handwriting. I show the students my own quick-write page and ask them to try to write at least one more line than they wrote the last time. I know they will naturally write more as we do this exercise every day; it never fails. But I have them focus on adding lines because it takes their mind off judging what they've written or going back to edit it. The idea is to get *more* material, not "correct" or "good" material. Eventually, when I put a prompt on the board most students will write for long periods of time. They love the spontaneity of writing without planning.

It never fails that a student will set his watch to beep at one minute. When the watch goes off, I tell students that I have a funny kind of clock that sometimes is fast and sometimes is slow. They should write as fast as they can in the time that they have. Then I give them the third prompt: "We never expected the weather that day to be. . . ." If they want to change the focus to food or work, they have complete freedom to do so. The prompts I use are so general that students can use them in many different ways. Figure 4–2 shows a number of prompts.

A Safe Place

After doing quick writes for a week or two at the start of the year, students become very good at developing details. One reason for this is that they know that the writer's notebook is a safe place for them to write. I don't ever read a notebook without the student asking me to do so. I ask them to write at least twenty pages in the notebook each quarter. At the end of the quarter, I ask each student to show me the notebook as well as other work. The student pages through the notebook as we count the pages together. I put a notation in the notebook and sign my initials and the date, and I do the same on the evaluation sheet that students bring to the front table with them. Twenty writer's notebook pages in ten weeks never seemed like a burden to me or to my students. If we do quick writes frequently, they have nearly that amount. As the year moves along, I don't have the class do the quick writes

Quick Writes

What she remembers is . . .	To be a great person, one has to . . .	Something from the past I'd like to bring back
When I was in eighth grade . . .	The day I was a hero . . .	How someone let me down
My first "crush" was on . . .	How I learned from failure . . .	A person I touched or who touched me
A prank that backfired . . .	A list of things I hate to eat . . .	How I took control of my life
When I let my emotions get the best of me . . .	The most awesome sight I have ever seen . . .	I felt as though I were in heaven when . . .
The time I felt good after a job well done . . .	A daily routine that I follow	An experience that taught me a lesson
The person I know who has had to overcome the most setbacks	Some skill few people know I possess	The neighborhood where I played as a child
I had to learn to go . . .	The day I saw the light	I could not breate I was so trapped
The one toy I cherished as a child	The greatest person I ever met	I wish I did not have this ordeal

FIGURE 4–2. *Quick Writes*

as frequently because I want them to become less dependent on me and to rely more on themselves to observe and write about the world around them.

The writer's notebook is also a safe place because I never make students read out loud things they have just written in it. Sometimes I read what I wrote, and sometimes I ask if anyone is willing to read what he or she wrote. Other times I ask students to turn to another person in the class and read part of what they wrote, or to just report about one of the three quick-write topics without having to read it. I don't do this very often, but if I do, it usually leads into some other activity. I mention ahead of time that I might be asking them to share something they've written. For the most part, the writer's notebook is personal, rather than private, and I allow writers to reveal their entries as they see fit. Perhaps this sense of safety is one reason students value the notebook so much.

Increased Appreciation

No matter what I say to students about how they might change their opinion about the use of the writer's notebook or even change themselves with its use, they have to experience it for themselves. Steve Dooley's reflection demonstrates his growing awareness of the usefulness of the writer's notebook:

> **The Writer's Notebook: Reflections on Reflections**
> **"A journal a day keeps the writer's block away."**
>
> In reflecting upon my writer's notebook, I see changes and growths, and entries ranging from the reminiscent to the light-hearted to the gravely serious. Although I don't really remember what my writer's notebook was like in 9th grade, I imagine this is a vast improvement.
>
> In the future, I hope to keep some kind of a diary or chronicle of my thoughts, modeled after my writer's notebook. In this book, I will be able to keep a clear record of my perceptions and of the seemingly ordinary, everyday occurrences that I encounter . . .
>
> I think that my very best entry did not originate off a quick-write, nor of my own thought but rather from something Mr. Mahoney said. This entry resulted simply from his stating that the purpose of the writer's notebook was to "record the ordinary." I did exactly this. In this particular four-page entry, I recorded the everyday characteristics of the three members of my immediate family. The reason that this entry is so important to me is because I know that in fifty years, I will not remember these types of things about those I love. I enjoy reading things like this that I wrote earlier in my life and I think that this is one of the ways that I truly do appreciate the writer's notebook . . .
>
> In all, throughout the school year, my appreciation of the WNB has increased tremendously. I no longer view it as just another

thing to do for English and as the school year ends, I intend to continue utilizing the concept of the notebook in the years to come.

One final lesson that my notebook has taught me is that things do not always come quickly or easily. It took me two entire school years to realize the importance of it, and now that I have, I am grateful for all the writing that we were forced to do. I hope in the future that I can continue to utilize this newfound tool.

One of the things that Steve's reflection teaches us is the value of patience. He suggests that he didn't fully understand or appreciate the use of the writer's notebook in his 9 Honors class. It wasn't as if I did any better job of introducing it than Jerry Matovcik had with the 9H class two years before. Nor was Steve slow to grasp things—he finished first in his graduating class. It just took time. In this age of quick fixes and knee-jerk reactions to tests and other data, we can take a lesson from students. Despite the number of times we say things, sometimes we need to let time take its course. Patience, while it doesn't come easily, grows out a faith in students' innate ability and desire to be literate if they are given genuine opportunities to write for real audiences and real purposes.

USING WRITING WORKSHOP

The Workshop's Structure

When I first started using a workshop approach, I divided the week into two days of writing (Monday and Tuesday) and two days of reading (Thursday and Friday). On Wednesday we could spend the full period doing work we needed to do as a whole class. We called Wednesday a "swing" day because students could swing from writing on the first two days to reading on the last two days. I didn't allow writing on the reading days or reading or writing literary letters on the writing days. Everything was compartmentalized. In time, I saw how arbitrary that was, particularly when a student was caught up in a book and wanted to continue reading on a day when it was "not allowed." I saw that some students were frustrated when they were closing in on a piece of writing and were told to put it aside because it was a reading day. Near the end of that first year, I announced that all days were reading and writing days.

I used to keep track with a clipboard of what each person was planning to do that period. I found using this "status of the class report" (Atwell 1987) after the minilesson too time-consuming, particularly in large classes, as it took at least five minutes a day. As I listened to students announcing their plans for the period, I had to write too fast, creating rushed and sloppy records, and I didn't always accurately hear what students said. I did, however, like the idea of knowing what students did each day. Instead of doing the writing myself, I passed the clipboard to the students, asking them to record what work they were currently doing and then pass the clipboard on to the next student. I found this useful as a double check of attendance as well as a reference for discussing students' progress to date.

Figure 4–3 shows a "status of the class" report created this way. The form I used could also serve as a record of the minilesson that I gave in each class. I left the clipboard on the side of the room in a basket and picked it up the next day. In some classes, at the beginning of the year I recorded what pages students had reached in their reading the night before. I listed just the title of the book they were reading, then simply added the page they were up to. It was a way of seeing at a glance how much reading students were doing each night. The whole process took no more than a minute and I often got the information as students were walking in the door before class, so no class time was lost. Later, when the clipboard went around the room, students recorded what they would be working on that period. All of this information was material that I could use when talking with parents about their child's work habits and progress.

Some of my students dubbed my minilessons as "maxilessons" for my tendency to turn them into something longer. In some classes, students love it when they can get the teacher off the topic and talking about something unrelated to their study. In my classes, students felt that they had work to do and any lesson I gave, long or short, was time taken from things they needed to accomplish. Sometimes I felt I needed just a short time (less than five minutes) to make a few announcements or show the class something, then they could move on to their own work while I spent the rest of the period having individual or small-group writing conferences.

After the minilesson, which normally took from ten to twelve minutes, students could do several different things. They could go to the library to get a book or to photocopy material, have a writing conference with me or with another student, go to the computer room to work on a piece of writing, or remain at their desks and continue their work. In some classes, I had a table in the front corner of the room where I would meet with students. In rooms where a table wasn't available, I would sit in the very back of the classroom and meet with students there.

There were periods of time, often weeks, when we would either start the class or end it with a student speaking to the whole class. Sometimes they would be celebrating a finished piece of writing or telling others about their current reading. They might be seeking feedback on a piece of writing, looking for a title suggestion or a reaction to a passage. We sometimes spent a day or two with students reading their writing aloud for all to hear and to appreciate. I saw the value of having students listen to and acknowledge the work of their classmates, but I also saw that this could be time-consuming and interrupt students who were just getting into a writing flow. Since I had to balance these two important issues, sometimes we would go for weeks without doing this.

When I had been giving longer-than-usual minilessons, I would make up for it by announcing that the next day would be a "silent" minilesson.

Status of the Class — English 8

LEFT HAND SIDE OF ROOM ROWS 1, 2, 3

Name	Monday JAN 4, 93	Tuesday 1/5	Wednesday 1/6	Thursday 1/7	Friday 1/8
1. Matt Ditewig	work on story	Working on Big Story (1st draft)	write lit. letter to Rob	give lit. let to Rob find Book to read	Start reading new book "Something Upstairs" pg I
2. John Mulligan	writers note books		LIBRARY		Read in Books
3. ~~Joan Hudson~~ ED HAMRAH	writers note Book	work on writers note Book (weekend)	work on my Dream weekend and what did it tell me	reading Uncle tom's cabin pg 140	write tom's cabin pg 150
4. Melissa Henn	writers notebook	writing notebook (vacation)	music lesson	reading pg 159 (Gone with the Wind)	computer room poem (Dream)
5. Kristen Lotito	finishing childrens story	computer room - poetry story	computer room	Peer Conference	computer room to type story
6. Amanda Seppi	finishing childrens book	computer room finish story	ending miniature wisegups computer room	peer conference	ab
7. Kristy Campo	writers Notebook	writers n/b poems	Working on poem "Destiny"	Lit Letter to Amy	Reading Never look back...
8. Amy Jaeger	writers notebook	work on poem	add last couplelines	Reading Last of the mohicans	reading mohicans P.137
9. Todd Seus	writers notebook	the war on villa Street LIBRARY	LIBRARY	villa Street Page 12	P147
10. Tim Kash	write notebook			Checkmate P.84	Checkmate P.95
11. Jennifer Tann	writers notebook	working on poems in my writers Notebook	computer room	reading! Maniac Magee	reading maniac magee by Jerry Spinelli pg 141 (just started)
12. Janelle Fedrich	writers notebook (POEM)	trying to think about something to write	music lesson rotation	writing a childrens book pg 122	computer room
13. Tracy Cozzolino	writers notebook (poem)	Tracy Cozzolino work on story	computer room	book - The Prince of Tidewater, by Gabriel Scott	reading - The Journals of Spoon Skurzynski pg 44
14. PATTERSON ERIN	work on new fiction story	work on a poem	rewrite poem I wrote yest.	went to library book/lit let.	ab

MINI-LESSON FOR THE DAY:

	Monday	Tuesday	Wednesday	Thursday	Friday
	GETTING BACK CHANGES W/O MR. C. STUD. TR	USING WRITING TOOLS - A GRAMMAR HAND-BOOK	SHOW ADRIENNE LU'S "SHELL FISHER"	USING EPI-GRAPHS -	TESTS OF CHARACTER - IN LIT. LTR.
	1. STATUS OF CLASS - PASSED AROUND	ALL RIGHT ALRIGHT ALREADY ALL READY A LOT AT LOT	WRITING FROM ANOTHER'S POINT OF VIEW	JOANNA GROGEL IN HER POEM -	LIST CHARACTERS IN BOOKS READ WHO HAVE HAD
	2. ATTENDANCE	P.537 - HOW DO YOU FIND OUT? TABLE OF CONTENTS? INDEX?		BLACK LIKE ME	TO PROVE THEM-SELVES
	3. LIT. LOG SHEET			NEEDFUL THINGS	
	4. WK #8 - 3 TO GO			ANNE OF AVONLEA	
	5. SHOWING BOOK I MADE FOR "MAHONEY MADNESS"	SPELLING - "WORDS OFTEN CONFUSED"			

FIGURE 4-3. *Status of the Class*

This meant that when we came to class the next day, we would maintain an atmosphere of silence from start to finish. I would write "Silent Minilesson" on the board, and would have nothing more to say publicly to the class. On such days, students were delighted that they had a full forty-three minutes to work uninterrupted by their teacher. It was always amazing to see how well they went right to their work and spent the time fully engaged. It was equally amazing to see how annoyed they became when their concentration was broken by an announcement on the PA or by a classroom visit from an administrator or other person.

Writing Conferences

Some teachers wonder how I found the time to teach and to have conferences. In a very real way, my writing conferences *were* my teaching. The one-on-one instruction was like a music lesson to fine-tune a musician. I would often start class with a minilesson that lasted from five to twenty minutes. I might show the students a parody, or how to slow a piece of writing down by having the main character become reflective. The minilesson might consist of having students use two absolutes at the start of a sentence to describe the subject, or use dashes in imitation of Emily Dickinson. There were scores of things that I could show the whole class quickly or could linger longer with. If one day I showed students how a particular writer used labyrinthine sentences, and the next day in a writing conference a student showed me a labyrinthine sentence, I might borrow the piece to make a transparency to show the work to all of my classes the following day. One thing I tried to do frequently was to use student writing as models in the minilesson.

After I finished the minilesson, I would meet with students who needed help with a piece of writing. Generally a student would ask for a conference and we would have it right on the spot. At the middle school, I often sat in the back of the room with an empty desk on my left. Students could slip in and out of the desk easily without climbing over the arm as they would have had to do if the empty desk were to my right. In high school classrooms, I usually had an empty table and two chairs in the front corner.

There has been much written about who holds the pen and paper. I did it both ways. Students would generally come to the table and sit to my right, making it easier for me to keep the paper between us and allowing me to write on the paper. Sometimes the student kept the paper and did the writing, particularly when the kind of feedback he or she wanted was clear and could be done simply by talking. The key is to have the student leave the conference wanting to write and eager to do more, even if it is to edit. The student has to want feedback for it to be effective. That's why I ask students to tell me what they want to happen from the conference. Untrained writers will say, "Just tell me if it's any good," forcing me to decide if they are looking for affirmation and a pat on the back or actually want complete honesty. Most writers want more positive statements than negative ones. That's why the best support is to use someone's work in a minilesson to demonstrate a particular skill or idea. After a piece has been used that way, its writer is generally interested in making it better.

Teach the Writer, Not the Writing

One way to solve the dilemma of how much correction should be done on a student's paper is to approach the issue from another direction. Ultimately, we want students to grow more independent of us. To help them do so, we have to focus on what the writer does well and needs to work on, rather than on what the paper needs in order to be correct. Papers come and go, but writers remain with us and it is they who need the attention. That is a hard concept to maintain in an "assign and grade" environment because the marking up of the paper is the justification for the appraisal of the work. I did plenty of that in my beginning years. I assigned a composition because it was about time for students to do another piece of writing and because I needed another writing grade, one every three or four weeks. In such situations, teachers treat student work as an appraiser would treat a piece at an art auction, telling the world how valuable the work is, pointing out its flaws as well as its strength. That's fine if the public is buying, but it's not so good when nurturing young writers. There is no need to point out every flaw of a piece for the student to improve, any more than a parent needs to point out every flaw to a young child trying to hit a ball with a bat. The point is to help the batter to hit the ball, not to justify an overall grade for hitting. If the parent is a good coach, he or she will adjust the pitching by tossing underhand, slowing the pitch down, or moving closer to the batter so that the child will hit the ball. A teacher does the same for each student, whether there are thirty in the class or ten.

Emphasizing Praise

Just as they say that there is no such thing as spoiling an infant with too much love and attention, I suggest that there is no such thing as too much praise. This goes for even the weakest writers—the ones who score the lowest on state assessments. The question is, what can they do *right*? That's the starting point. If my total load of students is low, I can maintain a writing conference record (WCR) for each one (Figure 4–4). If I have many students, I ask them to maintain this form for themselves. The WCR is simply a sheet of paper with a column for students to list the title and date of each piece they write, its genre or type, and the number of words. For each piece listed, I write two to four things that the student has done right in the second column, then two things the student needs to work on in the third column. If I am maintaining the WCRs, I update them while having student conferences. If students are keeping them, I write my comments on a separate piece of paper during conferences, then the students adds them to the form.

WRITING CONFERENCE RECORD FOR

◯ #

E.G. 11   Date _Fall 2000_   Name _____

Title of Piece & Date Type of Writing, # of words	Skills Used Correctly	Skills to Be Worked on Taught in Conference
(Student fills in this info.) Record these comments on your own sheets.		
1.		
2.		
3.		
4.		
5.		
6.		

FIGURE 4–4. *Writing Conference Board*

Depending on how much criticism students want and can handle, I try to put more in the "skills used correctly" column than in the "to be worked on" column. For some students, this may mean that I'm pointing out skills as seemingly basic as their ability to begin each sentence with a capital letter or begin each paragraph by indenting. The student who gets such a comment may say, "That's no big deal. Everyone knows that." I'll say that not everyone does, even in college. In the conference, I'll say, "Look, you knew enough to make a new paragraph because you were changing time or place or ideas. You were being kind to your reader by signaling that with a new paragraph. You gave the reader a signal by providing some white space and readers know that white space is a sign to blink or breathe or make a mental shift. Not all writers understand that, even if they unconsciously put the paragraphs in the right place. You have done that, and for those reasons." The student begins to understand that there are reasons for writing conventions, and something as simple as paragraphing can be a source of positive reinforcement—even for a struggling high school senior.

There are an infinite number of points to bring up for a range of students, depending upon their need. You could point out that a student has made a point and backed it up with a supporting sentence or two. That may be the place for a quick lesson to show how leading into the supporting sentences with a word that signals the transition would help. Even weak students can create some beautiful sentence structures. My structure favorite is the *absolute*. Without realizing exactly what he is doing, a student might write, "My shoulders aching, I struggle with the casket." Such a sentence might go right up on the board for the class to copy down in their writer's notebook, with the writer's name below it, or I might ask the student if I may use it in a minilesson the next day. I will take a sentence—or even a whole poem or paragraph—and make a transparency to use with all my classes, showing students what one student wrote and why it is so powerful. I'll then ask them to imitate this student by trying to create such a structure themselves, maybe in something they are currently working on. We'll listen to a few of the things students come up with and then move on, stopping to thank the first student for bringing such a sophisticated structure to our attention. Such recognition is worth a thousand As for students. Their work has been validated and they are eager to write more. Like small children batting, students enjoy the feeling of "hitting the ball" and are likely to want to get up at bat again.

MARKING AND GRADING

I have had many teachers tell me that the parents in their district would be up in arms if the teachers didn't find and mark all the mistakes in student papers. Some tell me that their principal or department chairperson has told them that they are to mark up the entire paper and find all of the mistakes.

Changing a teacher from evaluator to helper and guide involves quite a paradigm shift. Giving up the red pen does not come easily. I sometimes even now find myself slipping into old habits and looking to point out mistakes. I have to catch myself and remember that the paper is not the important thing, the writer is. I have to ask myself if I discouraged or helped to energize the writer. Getting away from taking piles of papers home to mark them in isolation was the best thing I ever did in making this paradigm shift. Not only did it free me from the never-ending pile of papers that I could never do justice to, but it also forced me to take time in class to work with writers. I could then spend my time at home writing responses to students' literary letters to me, a joyful and productive activity instead of a dreaded one.

As much as the writing conference is important, the attitude of the teacher is even more critical. I try to show genuine awe and admiration for what students can do. I've never found that I could give students too much praise. I might sometimes even write in a literary letter, "I hope you don't think I'm overdoing it when I tell you how good [some aspect of the writing] is. You are probably getting tired of hearing me say how much I like how you do some things. If so, just let me know." A little note like that reinforces my points in the writing conferences, and I've never had a student say, "You're right. I'm getting tired of hearing you say that." Such encouragement is quite different from a vacuous "Good job!" or "Well done!" or "Fantastic!," which doesn't tell students anything very helpful or let them know that a particular skill or section is effective. "Good job!" is like a dog getting a bone for a trick. If the dog has had enough bones, he will not perform the trick any more. Rewarding students with a "Good job!" or even an A+ is not helpful feedback. Instead, it is a reward for the writing, a focus that is not very effective in the long run.

Speaking of Grades

As a result of this paradigm shift, I gave up grading student writing. I knew that getting grades had never helped me, even in some graduate courses in writing. We never got grades on individual papers. We just got feedback from others in the class and from the professor. The desire to do well came from writing effective, honest pieces. The absence of grades allowed us to experiment, to take risks, to do things we might not have done if the piece were to be evaluated.

When I first gave up grading, students, particularly those in honors class, didn't understand how they could do a piece of writing and not receive a grade. The honors students had been weaned on rewards and many had been placed in the honors track because they had learned to give teachers what they wanted. When teachers ask me about not grading student writing, I ask them if they get graded on every class they teach or even on every week they teach. They admit they do not and that the closest they come to getting graded is a classroom observation once or more a year—sometimes not even that frequently. "Well, how do you get grades?" they ask, and we are onto another issue (discussed in Chapter 8, "Figuring Out Evaluation"). We can agree that grading students is not necessary to help them improve as writers and that grading writing is usually done to justify a report card grade.

Experimentation Is the Key

The process of assigning and grading takes up so much time for the teacher and the class that it limits the number of writing experiences a student can have. Once grades are no longer the major issue in developing pieces of writing, students are free to venture into a variety of genres—they can try poems, dramatic monologues, dialogues, double voice, labyrinthine sentences, parodies, and a full range of other forms. It is quite different from the "assign and grade" mentality that I used for many years of singling out a form—for example, the dramatic monologue—and ask all students to write a piece of that type, then to evaluate it and return it with a grade. To be fair to students, the teacher would need to prepare several models; go over all the characteristics of the monologue; provide some guided practice and time for feedback; set a reasonable date for the work to be handed in; and then read, evaluate, and return the work. All or most students might gain an appreciation for the dramatic monologue, but they would not have the opportunity to work in more than one mode. And many teachers are reluctant to assign one piece of writing until they have finished grading the prior assignment, adding even more time to the process.

When E-ZPass came into being in the New York area, drivers soon realized that they could avoid waiting in endless traffic lines to get through toll booths if they had a transponder that a machine could scan, automatically deducting the toll from an account. I began to see the toll booth as a metaphor for teachers who must take one piece of student writing at a time while others wait in line. The writer can't get through the toll booth until the teacher has collected the toll—marked the paper and returned it with the change necessary. Students and drivers both need to go about their business without slowing down for such "small-change evaluation." The student's "account" can be taken care of at the midway mark or at the end of a marking period simply by showing what has been done thus far. I've never had any students complain about this process, and most applaud it for freeing them up to write. I'm always reminded of Lucy Calkins' advice:

> If students are going to become deeply invested in their writing, and
> if they are going to draft and revise, sharing their texts with each
> other as they write, they need the luxury of time. If they are going
> to have the chance to do their best, and then to make their best better, they need long blocks of time. (1986, 23)

Letting students sponsor their own work and not evaluating them every step of the way became guiding principles for me.

SKILL BUILDING WITH SENTENCE COMBINING

Once I was a grammar nut. It's not that I learned grammar as a student—just the opposite. I knew hardly any grammar when I first began to teach, but since I knew so little else and had such poor preparation for teaching, I thought that I should teach some grammar to my ninth-grade students. I found a book that had the parts of speech, so I proceeded to teach that aspect of grammar. Over the next five or six years, I became fairly knowledgeable about grammar and tried to tie it in with "Composition Errors Illustrated," a ten-page handout I had been given in my freshman composition course in college. During these years, I taught lessons how to avoid comma splices, fragments, remote or vague pronoun antecedent references, and shifts in voice, tense, and mood, and other grammatical errors.

I came to discover that students didn't write any better for my lessons, and that I did very little instruction about how to write and a lot about what *not* to do. I began to experiment with having students manipulate clauses and sentences to say things correctly. Then in 1981, I went to Boston to my first NCTE conference. I also took part in a three-day workshop on sentence combining run by William Strong and Don Daiker. Suddenly, a whole world of style, grammar structures for writing, and other writing options opened up to me, including using participial phrases, absolutes, appositives, subordination, and other structures. I bought some of the books available at the time and worked with my students to develop their own stylistic options. I also worked these devices into my lessons and asked students to imitate these structures. Students began to notice these devices in the works they were reading, and they became more aware of the ways writers craft their work. I knew that my students' writing was improving in sophistication of structure and syntactic fluency, yet I had no tangible proof of this growth, even though there was much evidence in the professional books and journals that improvement was possible.

When New York State began its new assessment process in 1998, students in eleventh grade had to sit for a two-day exam consisting of four essays on different tasks. The essays were to be scored by teachers using five criteria and a 1 to 6 scale. The five criteria were *meaning, development, organization, language,* and *conventions.* Two teachers were to read each essay and give it a score. The two scores would be averaged. To help teachers score the exams, sample papers in each scoring range were provided, along with an explanation of each score. When I looked over the sample papers, I began to wonder what would be necessary to raise a low-scoring paper to a high score. I took a paper that was scored at level 3, which is just below passing, and I reworded the paper, adding no new information, just changing the sentence structure. I added some appositives, some parallel structure, and a participial phrase or two. Then I asked over two hundred people at four workshops that I gave to take a test. They read another level-3 paper on the same topic without knowing what the score was, then used the rubric provided for the

New York State assessment teachers to score the paper. All participants agreed that this paper was in the 3 range. As a result of that evaluation, they knew what a 3 paper looked like. Then they read my altered paper and attempted to score it using the same rubric. Overwhelmingly, the paper was given an average score of 5, with very little variation. One possible conclusion to be drawn from this is that teachers are influenced by stylistically sophisticated papers. Another is that by using certain stylistic devices in a paper, the meaning and organization—as well as the level of language—are improved. Whatever the reason, teachers judge the writing to be better.

My point in doing this experiment at the start of a workshop was to show the power of using several sophisticated structures: the appositive; the absolute; the participle; two adjectives following the noun; the introductory dependent clause; parallel structure with forms such as prepositional phrases and clauses; strong action verbs; and other elements. Harry Noden, in *Image Grammar* (1999), calls these structures "brush strokes." They are the same elements identified and incorporated into their books by others, like William Strong, Donald Daiker, and Don Kilgallon. Asking students to do some sentence-combining activities gives them practice with these stylistic devices. I would often reinforce these lessons by suggesting that students include some of the structures we looked at in their next piece of writing. At the same time, I would point out a passage or two from an appropriate text and we would discuss how the writer accomplished the effect. Students can imitate the style or structure in their writer's notebook, getting a feel for the accomplishments of the writer.

Students don't have to be taught grammar terms directly. They come to use the terms as they incorporate the structures into their writing. I asked students to identify some structures in their writing in their quarterly portfolios. They would do this by highlighting a structure they learned and then writing in the margin why this structure was what they said it was and why they thought it was effective. While some of this instruction was done in minilessons, some of it was done during writing conferences. There is no need to test students on grammar or give them endless worksheets. Students learn to write better by using more writing options. In the process, they learn grammar terms, including the names of some of the sentence structures.

I used many writing activities and approaches not described here. The remaining area is expository writing, sometimes called school writing, which usually involves writing about literature and excerpts from literature. Such writing is usually used for state assessments,. However, writing about literature need not be seen solely as school writing—nor need it be dull and lacking in voice. The same is true for essays, such as the personal narrative or the narration for exposition. In a personal narrative, the writer describes an event that was important to him or her. Eleventh grader Liz Quinn's "The Hardest Goodbye," the story of her grandfather's death and the impact it had on her, is a personal narrative. A narration for exposition is a little different because it attempts to tell a story to make one or more points. The story serves as the reference for a number of things the writer has come to understand or to realize. This is a perfect form for high school students to write in as they come of age, or as they revisit the events of earlier years with older eyes. The reflections that students do in their final portfolios are examples of expository writing.

The hardest type of writing for students to master is what I call the *literary analysis*. While they write literary letters all year and have their say about the books they are reading, the literary analysis asks them to think more fully about a piece of literature and to take a position on the ideas in it. We usually analyze poems because they are short and easier to manage than longer works, but occasionally we use a short short story. A literary analysis asks a student to develop a position and write a thesis statement or a controlling idea on an aspect of a work we've read and discussed together. I do not ask my eighth graders to do this, but I do expect it from my tenth, eleventh, and twelfth graders. Eighth graders could be trained to write a literary analysis, but the time it would take for them to master the form isn't worth it when there are so many more interesting things for them to write about at that age.

5 | MAGIC WORDS

There are some occasions when poems or poetic prose pieces just seem to write themselves. My English teacher friend Bill Picchioni has an activity that he shared with his students to get them to appreciate the sensuous quality of words. He went through books of poetry looking for "magic words"—lush words, words that evoke a sensual appeal. He wrote the words on a sheet of paper, spacing them apart so as not to link them to the other words around them (Figure 5–1). He asked students to read through the list until a word resonated with some particular image they had, then to begin to write from that word. When they finished writing, students were to return to the list for more words. When they thought they were finished writing from the words, they could return to the work and begin to shape it and craft it into something meaningful to others.

I found immediate success with this lesson in my own classrooms. No matter what the grade or level of the class, students could find words to carry their images and create pleasing texts. I have tried this with students from second grade to sixth grade with equally great results. When I used this lesson in my son Brian's fifth-grade class in Florida, a couple of his difficult students became so excited at this exercise that they came back early from recess to work on their poems and to have me read them.

My student Jeanine Beatty wrote two poems using the magic words, then wrote a reflection on the two poems that she included in her portfolio.

Spilling Fire

Swift and sweet the
smooth,
slick hate
drinks the nectar of love
as death's sting radiates
off the spilling fire
of your voice.

Poetic Words & Phrases

by William T. Picchioni,
Lynbrook Schools

sweet   spontaneous   snow spring   darling

buds   angry   garden of   earth   spinning

pushing   yellow   blue birth   again   now   ground

wind   knife   moment   God   bright   the sound of

trees   groan   living   flame

tulips   deep dark gold   and love and lovers   naughty

dimpled   dappled   the wide wild embrace   furious

rosebuds   in triumph   damp   wet loam   curling

sprinkled   fingers   wolf and swan   stars   rhythm

juice

passion   homeless   time and time again   listen to the   ashes of

youth

fire   nourish   twilight   angels   the dead   answer

blue star   wingbeats   nights   sang the sun   in flight

the kiss of emerald   ancient incense   deception   O O Muse

blaze coolly   whiteflowinggossamergowns   return

the gift of grass and meadows and wildflowers all   swift and sweet

the grit of city streets swirling   in secret   drink   horrid   black-

ness

dreamily dream   gloom   softly   body curve   snake

scent

in darkness dwelt   ruined feathers   marble words   faith   on this

bed

the time of hurt   now and forever   cold canyon   like a steady en-

gine

in the wilderness   snarl of stones   blue white yes   the good the

rich

FIGURE 5–1. *Poetic Words and Phrases*

Venomous screeches of distrust and anguish,
fear and fallacies,
condescension and contempt,
burn tender skin
exposed to scorching commentary.

Friendly War

Her usually composed face
shifted into an unrestricted grin:
The sisters engage in friendly war,
tugging and pushing,
attempting to thrust the other
into the sheet of blue-white cold.
Flecks of green dance
in pairs of identical eyes
and fiery bliss radiates from
childish deeds.
Footing lost,
feeble arms and legs swing
in attempt to regain balance.
To no avail.
Icy glacial water
cascades over the raven hair and ivory limbs
of ecstatic youth.

Reflecting on "Spilling Fire" and "Friendly War"

Since I used the same technique to write each of these poems, I decided that it would be appropriate to place them on the same page and use one reflection.

One day during the first quarter, Mr. Mahoney introduced a way to add some variety to our writing by using a sheet of words taken from different sources of literature. "Spilling Fire" wasn't originally about anything in particular; I just took some of the words and put them together, or as Mr. Mahoney would say, I "went with the surprise." When I got to the end, and used my own description, I decided that it would be about hate or the "spilling fire of your voice." Originally, this poem was longer, but I decided to cut a lot out of it because it really didn't make sense and I thought it would be better if the majority of the poem was made up of my own words rather than a copy of another person's ideas.

The second poem, "Friendly War," came in the fourth quarter. I had run out of things to write about at that point, so the minilesson came just in time. I decided to write this poem about two girls, sisters, playing near the water. I found that the second time that I attempted this exercise I didn't use as many of the words from the sheet; I felt that I was more creative with this piece.

In general, I like the technique as a change of pace, but I don't think I would want to use it frequently. It made me feel like I am stealing. Of course, that is ridiculous because nobody can own words. A good thing about this is that it brings out the best in my writing, in terms of description. I read through the poems and I realized that even though it seemed like all of the words were from the sheets, in reality very few of them were.

THAT WRITING STATE OF MIND AGAIN

When students have ownership of their work, the things they do reverberate and they keep coming back to them. Because of her experience with "Spilling Fire," Jeanine later wrote the poem "To Whom It May Concern" and reflected on it in her portfolio.

To Whom It May Concern

Your whispers weave through my soul.
Scarring my emotions,
Burning, aching,
they consume me.
Insignificant comments,
disregard for my feelings.
When to my face they are in jest,
but are not harmless,
I distance myself,
ignoring my pain,
the hollow pit in my stomach,
Attempting to ignore your
stabbing remarks.
You may say that I overreact.
If I am not accurate,
If I am not really appreciated,
Bring it to my attention.
Sometimes I just need to hear it.

Reflecting on "To Whom It May Concern"

I can honestly say that this is one of the most important poems to me because of all the emotions that I was feeling at the time that I wrote it.

More than once in my life I have felt like I care more about other people than they do about me. This is especially the case with some of my "friends." Even though I wrote this poem about people talking about other people behind their backs, it could be taken to mean other things. I realized after "To Whom It May Concern" was completed that, along with "Spilling Fire," it could be used to show feelings of anybody who has ever been ridiculed for any reason. Everybody needs to know that they are appreciated once in a while.

In situations such as these, I especially love writing because it allows me to express all of my feelings and realize that it might not be as bad as it seems.

MAKING CONFESSIONS

Sometimes I've shown students my writing about regrets I have in my life. I refer to these pieces as *confessions* and as a way of seeking forgiveness from some of the people I've hurt or neglected. Such writing may be good to share with another person, or it may be helpful simply to write it. It may be the first step in mending fences. I've shown students a poem I wrote about my father, who died in 1973.

Left Behind

My father's feet were always lame, slowing him down.
even when I was ten,
and he once played a baseball game down in the back field,
whacking one way out near the weeds,
and then hobbling around the bases.
But that was before I began to distance myself from him.

"I got bum feet," he would say,
And it seemed he was always going to the chiropodist.
He would start out for the seven block walk
to church on Sunday mornings,
ten minutes ahead of my mother,
who would arrive at the same time that he did.

"Slow down," he calls out to me.
He can't keep up.
I walk ahead, rushing almost,
through all the parking lots and walkways
to Shea Stadium.
He tries as best he can
but he can't keep up.
"Jimmy, wait up," he pleads,
but I, some thirty years younger,
look annoyed at him,
driving him harder to try to catch up.
"We want to get to batting practice before it's over,"
I say over my shoulder,
but I'm really the one who wants to get there, not him,
and so I ignore his pleas and push on,

even on his 60th birthday,
the day we have given him a gift
of taking him to the ball park.

Using my example, students are free to write for a few minutes in their
writer's notebook. Of course, many choose not to write such confessional
work, but some do, even showing it to me in a conference. Because of the delicate nature of this kind of work, I have chosen not to include any student examples here. However, such writing goes far in healing old wounds and
repairing damage done. For many of my students, this writing serves a real
purpose and it "goes somewhere" other than into a folder in the teacher's desk.

TRANSITIONAL WORDS

One way to bring to the consciousness of students the importance of transitional words is to show them how such words can shape a story or a short
poem. I wrote the two poems that follow using four particular words or
phrases. I then asked students to write their own poems, using my words or
substituting their own.

Stunning Turnarounds

Sometimes
    My students appear to be so thick
    And can't seem to understand my lessons
    And fail to do the work that seems so simple,
And often
    They stare at me with glassy eyes
    Or frown at me as if I have three heads,
And usually
    I start to think the same
    And go ahead and check the mirror,
    Wondering if I can ever make a dent,
But then
    Out of nowhere
    One seems to get it
    And then another and another,
    And before I realize it
    I am amazed once more
    At the powerful voices of my students.

Winter Wipeout

Occasionally
    When the snow comes ripping out of the north
    And threatens to bury us in waist-high drifts,
    And howls its flakes against our panes, we

Frequently
>> Grow excited . . .
>> And dream of snow closings and days off,
> And usually
>> We get ourselves so convinced of our liberation
>> We let tomorrow's school work
>> Drift from our minds
>> And bury itself under mounting snow,
> But just then,
>> Like a TV being flicked off by some remote clicker,
>> The snow stops cold,
>> And we are left with our frozen dreams
>> And no school work done for the next day.

Angel Lloyd, like most of the students, was able to write a poem using the transitional words and phrases.

Untitled

Sometimes
>> We rush forward in our lives
>> And try to speed the aging process
>> Until we get to a certain point.
> And often
>> When we get there,
>> We try to stay there
>> And stop the aging process—
>> Until we look back on our silliness.
> And usually
>> We wish we'd lived our fleeting lives
>> Differently,
> But sometimes
>> It's too late.

Angel led an interesting discussion with the class about the way students look at time and how they keep rushing ahead without enjoying the moment.

DEALING WITH DEATH THROUGH POETRY AND PROSE

One of the hardest things teenagers have to deal with is the death of a someone they love, often a grandparent but sometimes a close friend. Young people are often described as believing they are invincible and that death will never touch them. When people close to them die, a teenager's world is shaken violently. My friend Jerry used "The Portrait" by Stanley Kunitz to explain to his class that sometimes we cannot write about painful things right away and must let some time pass. He explained how Kunitz experienced an incident with his mother when he was very young: He was so hurt by her reaction to his finding a picture of his father, a suicide victim, that her slap to his face still stung him when he recalled it sixty-four years later. At that point, though, Kunitz could finally write about it. Later that day when Jerry was on cafeteria duty, Kyle Rouggley, one of his students, came up to him and said that he thought he was going to write about his father's death. Jerry cautioned him that he didn't have to and that Kunitz had to wait a long time before he could deal with his painful memories. Kyle said that he understood, but that he thought he was ready to deal with his father's death.

Several weeks later, the class was listening as students volunteered to read something they had written recently or were currently working on. At Kyle's turn, a few students urged him to read about his father, but Kyle didn't want to. They persisted, saying how good it was. Jerry told him that if he wanted to read it, he could, and to consider this a safe place to do so. Kyle said, "Okay, I'll read it, but if I cry, it's your fault." He then read "The Day," in which he describes the funeral of his father, who died when Kyle was in elementary school. He tells of the grief of his mother and sister and how he cries silently to himself. He also mentions how relatives remember Kyle's father and how Kyle looked when he was younger. He wonders if the tears he swallows are for his sister and his mother or for himself. As he says his last goodbye, he wants to reach out and touch his father. He thinks he sees his father's chest moving, but then considers it wishful thinking. Kyle finishes by telling of the final act, the folding of the flag that is on the coffin. He mentions that he and his father had folded the flag together every day as a ritual. When he sees the folded flag he bursts into tears and knows for sure that his father is dead.

When Kyle finished reading with tears in his eyes, there was a hush over the whole class. No one spoke, no one moved. Jerry remained silent as well. After about a minute, he said that they should all think of that period of silence as a tribute to Kyle's father and as recognition of how his son had recorded a painful memory.

There are three important topics that arise with Kyle's poem. The first is that it is very difficult for a teacher to break away from the traditional setting of a teacher-driven or a packed, curriculum-driven approach to English. If every day and every lesson is tightly planned out, there is little opportunity for teacher or students to figure things out. If a teacher does break away from the standard operation, all too often she will return soon because of pressure from colleagues or superiors, or a sense of the isolation and uncertainty of traveling in uncharted waters. I was fortunate to have in Jerry a fellow traveler who could reassure me when I doubted and who I could remind, when he needed reassurance, of the great things he was doing with his students. Time after time, teachers return to the old ways because of a lack of support from those around them. It takes a community to help create a literate environment in a classroom and in a school.

In the case of Kyle and his poem, this is how sharing and having a confidant worked for Jerry and me. During a free period later that day, Jerry showed me Kyle's poem, having asked him for permission. When I read the poem, I asked Jerry for a copy to show to my classes that afternoon. One result of such sharing in a school population of about eight hundred is that students will tell other students that they heard or read something of theirs in their English class. This is one way of having writers be acknowledged for their work outside their own classrooms. In the cafeteria or in passing at a locker, a student might well say to Kyle, "Mr. Mahoney showed us your poem in our English class today. That was beautiful the way you described it. I really loved that. I think I'll write something about my grandmother's death." This genuine sharing creates a safe environment in which a person can express deep emotion without being ridiculed or treated oddly.

Jerry and I noticed the sophisticated sentence structure and literary devices that Kyle had used without being knowledgeable about the names for such things. In a minilesson to my students, I showed them the lines "My mind numb with grief,/I cry." The first thing Kyle did was use an absolute, which is a modifying structure that looks almost like a sentence but lacks a complete verb. Usually the state-of-being verb is dropped out. Kyle might have said, "My mind is numb with grief and I cry." The second thing he did was to show his own isolation by putting himself on a line by itself, away from his mother and sister. This is an example of what I tell students is "FFF"—"form follows function." Kyle used the form of isolation to show his own feelings of being alone. He went one step further by using two single-syllable words that happen to rhyme: "I cry." When students see how one of their own friends has created such a heartfelt poem but has used a tool of the writer's craft to do it, they begin to see how important it is to both write from the heart and work at crafting their writing.

A ninth grader, Mary Zoccoli, did just what Kyle had done when she tried to capture her special memories of her grandmother.

Vivid Images

The vivid images come every so often.
I see her smile,
I hear her laugh,
I feel her love and comfort.
I thought she'd always be here to reach out a hand and tell me
she cares.

There she sits, listening to my problems.
She's fading away—vivid images.
So vivid,
Transparent.
She's actually gone.
Where did she go?

To that place in the sky?
I wonder if I will ever know.
Did she stay with me?
I believe so—vivid images.

I touch her hand.
I know she's watching over me.
All this time—vivid images

Her hands are cold and bony white.
She's drifting closer toward me.
Now I understand
She's deep in my heart,
Down in my soul,
Walking with me, hand in hand—vivid images.

Other students in my classes followed Kyle's lead and wrote about their own painful memories, working through their grief in this way. Each year, Jerry and I used Kyle's poem in a minilesson, showing the Stanley Kunitz poem and telling the Kyle story. A year or two after Kyle wrote his poem, we experienced what so many high schools do—a student dying tragically in a car accident. Over spring vacation, a popular tenth grader, Brian Healy, died in just such a way. In class we gave students an opportunity to write about Brian, first by showing them Kyle's poem, then by remaining quiet and giving them time and space to grieve in their writing.

Corey Cherouvis, a tenth grader and, like Brian, a football player, wrote a poem called "The Hardest Day" about Brian's funeral, describing how he and seven other friends pull Brian's casket from the hearse and carry it up toward the church doors. It is only in that action that Corey has a clear realization that he is actually carrying his friend's body. He notices that everyone is staring at them as they come down the aisle, causing his friends and him to fight back tears. After they place the coffin on the stand and return to their seats, Corey begins to cry softly and a woman in the pew behind him responds to his emotion by rubbing his back in comfort. In his tears, Corey remembers his friend Brian and realizes how important life is.

For Corey, this truly was a very hard day. He had to deal with his friend's death and confront his own mortality. The previous year, he had been a student in my ninth-grade English class when I presented a minilesson using Kyle's poem "The Day." The following spring, Corey was again my student, this time in an English 10 class, when news of Brian Healy's death came so abruptly. As the school mourned the loss of a popular student, I talked in class about ways to express emotion over death, and as an example I used Kyle's poem. I pointed to Kyle's use of the absolute and other elements. Corey decided to imitate some of Kyle's techniques, so he too used the line "I cry" and set it off by itself. He also used the absolute structure in the lines "We walk down the aisle, everyone staring at us,/While we fight back tears." He subordinated the words "everyone staring at us" so that it is a detail in the form of an absolute but it is secondary to his walking and fighting tears, the idea that makes this the hardest day. He even borrowed from Kyle's title and added his own adjective, "hardest." Corey ended with a realization, just as Kyle did. Kyle accepted that his father was truly dead and that he had to face that reality. Corey came to realize through his friend's death that life is very precious and needs to be treated with care.

Perhaps the lessons that students learn in cases like these are only crystallized when they write about them. In doing so, they come to connect even more deeply with their feelings while they use the writings of others, including fellow students, as guides. As teachers, we need to allow opportunities for students to deal with their powerful emotions, but we also need to present them with tools to allow them to craft pieces that will stand as good writing long after their grief has subsided.

Eleventh grader Erin Powers first wrote a poem about her longtime friend Brian Healy, then she wrote a final tribute to him for the literary magazine and for the poetry reading later that spring.

Brian

Why am I kneeling beside you,
Your eyes closed for an eternity,
Face pale as the white "73"
On your fire-red jersey?
Please sit up
And laugh with me.
Dry my eyes.
Give me assurance.
Where are you?
Can you see me?
Are looking up at me through
Shut eyes,
Or down from heaven
Crying in bright sunshine?
I don't want to cry
Because you might hear my sobs,
My choking breath,
And feel my pain.
I wish you were here
But most of all . . .
I wish you happiness.

One of Brian's closest friends was Jody Shenn, a fellow tenth grader at the time of Brian's death. Jody, like Erin, wrote a piece in tribute to his friend. In the process, he defined for himself the meaning of true friendship as he attempted to figure out how such a good friend could be taken. Jody and Erin both worked out some of their deep feelings through writing and then celebrating their friend's life with public readings.

DRAMATIC DIALOGUES AND MONOLOGUES

There are many genres in writing that are not so apparent to students, such as the dramatic dialogue, a type of writing introduced in *Writing with Passion* by Tom Romano (1995). Romano included a piece, called "Looking for Love," that was written by one of his former students, Marcia Stapleton Snively. In the piece, the writer presents an argument against sex before marriage in a dramatic way, by having a couple argue about the issue. Romano's point in having students write in this genre is that he wants students not just to present an intellectual position but to render it in a dramatic fashion. I showed some examples to my students and then asked them to try this. John, a senior and a student in the special education program, worked out his problem with getting only limited playing time on a school team by writing this dramatic dialogue:

The Confrontation

Coach: Let's call it a day. Hit the showers.

John: Mr. Dell, can I speak with you?

Coach: Sure, John. Meet me in my office.

John: Mr. Dell, I have something I need to ask you.

Coach: What's on your mind?

John: We have played eight games now and are half way though the season. I'd like to know how come some other players and I have not seen a minute of game time.

Coach: I play my best players.

John: I can't speak for the other players. However, I can speak for myself. I have come to every practice. I made every practice when you had double sessions. I always give 120+ percent and always do what you ask. I don't just do the drills but always try to improve my skills during the drill.

Coach: I know you work hard. I know you try. All I ever promised you and any of the other players was a uniform if you made the team.

John: I remember what you said but I think I am as good as some of the other players that have been given playing time.

Coach: I think they are a little better than you.

John: I know I may not be a star but I don't see much of a difference between me and some of the players that are playing.

Coach: That's why I am the coach. I make the decisions based on what I see.

John: What can I do to prove to you that I am equal to the other players that are given game time?

Coach: John, keep on trying and you may get your chance.

John: Coach, I'm not asking to be a starter although I certainly would want to be a starter. I am just asking for some playing time, especially when we are down by 3 or 4 goals with 5 or 10 minutes left. I want to prove to you that I can play the sport.

Coach: Go take a shower; I'll see you tomorrow.

John: Thanks, coach.

I covered up the writer's name and any references in the text to his identity, then showed the dialogue to the class to let them see how the writer presented a very important issue in a clear but dramatic way. One result was a lively discussion about playing time and the purpose of sports programs in school. Since there is no reference to a particular sport, girls as well as boys could examine the issues openly and discuss their own experiences and views. By seeing such an example, students can more easily create a dialogue on an issue that they are facing with a teacher, parent, friend, or relative.

It's a short leap from a dramatic dialogue to a dramatic monologue. Browning's "My Last Duchess" and Eliot's "The Love Song of J. Alfred Prufrock" are just two of many available models. One difference with this approach is that students are looking at the work of other artists so that they can figure out which genre might best serve their needs and how a particular artist accomplished the craft. I ask all students to begin some work in the poetic form; if they choose not to complete the work it's okay, but they must at least try. These efforts go into the writer's notebook, where the student can return to them later.

EARLY MEMORIES

Each year Jerry and I repeat a lesson that takes several days and yields rich rewards, including showing students how to get in touch with early memories. We have adapted it many times over but basically it deals with asking students to find a comfortable position at their desk, close their eyes, relax all their muscles, and go back far into the past to a period of great emotional feeling. With the lights off and their eyes closed, I ask the students a series of questions about the memory that alerts the five senses. I ask students to dwell in this moment for a good five to ten minutes. Then I ask them to slowly open their eyes, become accustomed to the classroom environment again, and then, in their writer's notebook, to write as rapidly as they can about all of the sense details that they can remember.

At this point, most students are writing prose. After five to seven minutes, I ask them to read over what they wrote, edit it for gaps, and read or tell about their incident to another student. This second student's job it is to ask about anything that's missing or confusing, and to point out to the writer any examples of strong sense details. The class period is usually over by this time.

The next day, I show students, using examples on the overhead, how to take a prose piece, cut out the nonessential parts, and then arrange the words into poetic form. I show them how to use the slash to indicate where they might want to break a line, how to punctuate the lines, and when to make a new stanza. I tell them that I find it useful to avoid having more than one strong image on a line. I also show them how to break a line to isolate a word or phrase for emphasis. For some students, this may be the first lesson of a practical nature that they've received on writing and arranging lines into poetic form. In the days that follow, they work on this poem, we conference on it, and they read their poems to others. Over time, they will use this process again and again.

Jackie O'Connor wrote this early memory about the birth of her brother, Mike, and his intrusion into her life.

Rebirth

I hear my brother wailing,
high pitched voice knifing
the stagnant, ammonia-filled air.
With every breath, his ruddy face
heightens with brilliant color.
Tiny fists knotted,
he shakes with each cry.
My family crowds for a glimpse
of the angelic face.
Pouting, I find little sweet
about the wrinkled, blanketed mass.
Bending, mom hums to the
now silent form in her arms—
soothing songs of my youth.
The camera flashes and
Abruptly snaps me out of my reverie.
Ever slowly, I trudge to the bedside
and peer into the helpless blue eyes.
Trapped in their cloudy depths,
I am more confused now than ever.
I am that child again,
the doubts and insecurities—
monsters I cannot escape.
I am given more attention now than ever,
yet, through it all, I can't help but wonder—
Will they love me less
now that I am no longer the baby?
Finally I make myself
hold the little baby
who's turned my world upside down
by simply being.
As he snuggles in
the warm crook of my arm
the bitter jealousy melts
into spellbound wonder.

Countless other students wrote about their early memories, some to elicit vague recollections from a long time ago and others to celebrate or mourn times that have stayed with them but were never put into writing. Liz Quinn wrote the following reflection about her prose piece on remembering her grandfather's death:

Reflection on "The Hardest Good-bye"

I'm really glad I had the opportunity to write this piece, and when I think of it, this piece had to be one of my favorite pieces this year—it certainly was my most personal. This started off as a class exercise in the beginning of the year. We had to recall a memory from our childhood and write a poem or prose piece about it. I remembered a very traumatic part of my childhood—the death of my grandfather. The events were so vivid in my mind but I never really had an opportunity to express them. This exercise provided such an outlet.

I do feel that parts of this piece sound a bit childish, but in a way, I feel that adds to the work. Because I was only seven when my grandfather passed away, I remember the events through a child's eyes, which explains why, at certain points, my reactions to the events occurring sound insensitive. I tried to add my experience and the knowledge I've gained to enhance the piece and provide a window into how I feel now, as opposed to how I reacted at the time. Overall, I'm very pleased with this piece. I'm glad I had an opportunity to relay my feelings.

WRITING AS TRIBUTES AND GIFTS

In more than twenty-five years of teaching before I started using the writing/reading workshop approach, I can't remember a single student writing something in my English class then giving it as a gift. In 1990, our dog Coco had to be put to sleep. I'll never forget the gloomy drizzle that fell that evening as my son Tim and I carried Coco into the vet's office to have her euthanized. I have never been very fond of dogs, but my wife had the good sense, over my slight protests, to have dogs as the kids grew up. Coco became Tim's dog when he was only nine and was his constant companion. She played soccer with him all the time, letting him kick balls at her as she guarded the net. In time she learned to chest-trap the ball, to field high kicks, and to dribble the ball back to where Tim stood. She is perhaps partly responsible for his development into a very fine soccer player—he got a partial soccer scholarship to college and captained the team for two years. Coco also played in all the neighborhood games out in the street, racing around in touch football games, guarding the net in street hockey, and chasing after tennis and Wiffle balls when they went astray.

The day Coco was scheduled to be put to sleep, my older son Brian got the bad news at work in a Florida office. He sat at his desk and wrote a poem that he eventually sent to us in New York.

The Last One in for Supper

Informed at work
By a "While You Were Out,"
The distance seemed much further
Than 'long distance.'
"Your dog," it said, "Call home."

Recent Christmases,
Like Dickens' final Ghost,
Had promised this; the
Howard Hughes routine,
Beneath a blanket in the corner
Of the furthest room,
The leglessness, the sniping
At fleas that weren't there.

Today, another childhood
Is harder to keep track of,
Like whiffle balls of last at-bats,
Landing somewhere in the aging dusk,
While mothers and streetlights
Announce supper.

She tended nets, she
Tripped up undisputed touchdowns, she
Fielded whiffle balls no one could see,
Padding down the block to save
The game before it rolled
Into the sewer.

She was the last one in for supper,
Always. While I was out, she padded
Off, down the block,
Out of distant streetlight's
Age old limit, into
The God-forsaken school night.

She left a man two thousand miles
Away, pretending to work late,
Crying at his desk for more at-bats
Against the God-forsaken school night,
Unable to come home for supper.

My wife loved Coco deeply and she loved the poem that Brian had written. She asked me to type it up and put it on fancy paper so she could have a nice copy of it. I did that in May of that year. Still Eileen wasn't satisfied. Though not skilled at desktop publishing herself, she knew that I could do something more, perhaps placing a photo somewhere on the paper. At the time, I didn't quite know how to do it, nor did I have the time to learn.

Months passed and we were well into the new school year. Things were humming in the workshop as I passed the guidance office one day and noticed Jerry with one of his ninth-grade students, Chris Dodorico. They were bending over a piece of paper and cutting something out with a special knife from the art room. Chris was cutting out a circle from the center of the paper. I asked what they were doing and Chris told me they were preparing a hole in the paper to mount a picture behind it. He was making it for his father as a Christmas present. Then he showed me that he had written a poem for his father and had drawn a circle in the center using PageMaker. That was the guide for what he was cutting out. He then placed the picture behind the paper to show the framed picture in the center of his poem. I was amazed at the effect and knew that this was what I could do for Brian's poem about Coco.

On Christmas Eve morning, I sat down at the computer and started in. I found three pictures—of my wife, the dog, and Tim—so I prepared three copies of Brian's poem. I bought picture frames, then wrapped the poems up for the next morning. Amidst piles of beautifully wrapped presents all around the room where we gathered with our three children and their spouses, my wife sat quietly in a chair and took great enjoyment in the *oohs* and *ahhs* of the gift-opening ritual. We had to urge her again and again to begin on her own pile. And still she sat. I was eager to have my two sons receive their poems, so I handed my wife the present with her copy in it so she could read it first. She opened it and then in silence looked at the picture and read the poem over and over again to herself. With tears running down her face, she said in a low voice so that only I could hear, "This is one of the best Christmas presents I ever received."

In time, I began to ponder why this gift was so special. For one thing, it was a gift created by both my son and me. Second, this work would be a constant reminder of what a great dog Coco was. Finally, it was a way of connecting our family in pictures and in words to our memories of Coco. I brought the picture into school after the vacation, almost having to promise my life in exchange for taking the frame down from the wall in the den. I showed the work to students and read them the poem. I also told them that I had been taught this technique by a ninth grader, Chris, and his teacher. I think it was important for me to mention the lesson I had learned because I was realizing again and saying to students that we need each other to help us figure these things out. In the weeks that followed, I saw a run on dog poems, accompanied by pictures. But I also saw tributes about departed grandparents or other relatives. Students often presented these works to one of their own parents, often the child of the grandparent who had died. These gifts were tearfully and joyfully received. Real writing had gone somewhere.

Why do we write, anyway? And why do we think it is so important that students be able to write well? One of the reasons is that we feel a need to compose our lives, to write about the life we live and have lived. We write to make sense of our life as well as to honor aspects of it. Jerry and I give a great deal of attention to real writing that goes somewhere—authentic writing. One of the areas we give valuable time to is what we call "Writing As Gifts."

Most of us can recall a child around kindergarten age—either ourself or a family member. The scene contains a parent, grandparent, or other member of the family greeting a child who runs off the school bus or comes racing in the door waving a drawing from school. The child is full of glee and races up to the older person, presenting the work as a present. It may be a crude drawing, a picture with some text, even a greeting card for a special occasion. The person receiving the work hugs the child, accepts the gift, then holds it out for admiration. After being further admired and shown around at home, the work gets hung up in a place of prominence, perhaps a bulletin board or the refrigerator. There is no mistaking the fact that the child's work has been given value. Though the work may remain up only a short while, it may end up in another place where such treasured gifts of love are kept: a scrapbook, a special folder, a drawer, a box. This work is real enough to be kept somewhere special. There's usually no grade on this work—such a mark would be entirely irrelevant to the receiver.

Why does such real writing stop when students get into upper elementary school or into secondary school? Why has authentic writing been replaced in the curriculum by school writing? Is it any wonder that the energy the artist has as a child disappears when all writing is assigned and is meant almost entirely for the teacher? The child has lost his autonomy as he moved up the educational ladder.

We think it is very important for students to write for an authentic purpose, and giving a gift is such a purpose. If we allow older children to write for a genuine purpose, they will drink at a well that will sustain them through some of the other kinds of writing they will be asked to do in secondary school.

Steve Dooley wrote the poem "The Myth" about his maternal grandfather's death eleven years before, when Steve was only six.

The Myth

Waiting—
The scent of a doctor's office,
My thought confirmed.
I wasn't allowed in
But Mom was.

The drive back was long and hot—
Practicing counting my numbers,
I was unaffected.

I knew then,
Death, a part of life.

The funeral was another day—
The room a coffin.
I walked to the front,
Dad lifted me—
I touched Grandpa's forehead.

One lesson we repeat each year centers on Seamus Heaney's "Mother of the Groom," a lovely poem about holding on and having things slip out, about rings and celebrations, about looking back and looking ahead. We ask students to try to imagine a person they care deeply about and to remember something special about that person. Instead of saying "I remember," we ask them to use a pronoun in the third person, such as *he* or *she,* to represent themselves, the writer. Students discover that using the third person gives them a sort of safety or shelter to say things they might not be able to say in first person. In the process, they learn a lesson about narrative point of view that's far more valuable than what they could have learned from simple definitions and tests.

Jeff was one of many students who wrote this kind of poem and then gave it as a gift. He first gave the poem to his mother, and then he made it the opening page in his portfolio, in effect dedicating his portfolio to his mother. The title of his portfolio is *Into the Void* and everything revolves around the theme of recognizing voids in his life and ways of filling them.

"You'll Always Fit"

What he remembers is . . .
    the constant caring,
    never putting herself before him,
    telling him, "You'll always fit,"
    not understanding how much more that meant.
What he knows is . . .
    that she will always be there for him,
    if he is sad, lonely, or just in need of an ear.
    He knows how proud she is of him,
    because she is his mother.
What he doesn't tell her is . . .
    that nothing she does goes
    unappreciated,
    that he will always be there for her,
    that he is proud of her,
    and that he loves her.

> *You've filled the void like none other.*
> *So this is for you, Mom. You'll always fit.*
> I love you.

Jeff told the story behind this poem in a reflection in his quarterly portfolio. When he was little, his mother used to read to him in a particular chair where the two would sit together. As Jeff got older, sometimes he would seek a different chair or want to sit on the floor because he thought it would be too tight a squeeze and that he "didn't fit anymore." His mother told him that no matter what happened, he would "always fit" with her. Jeff's gift was to return this affirmation years later in his tribute to his mother. We can bet that no grade on this poem would have any bearing for either Jeff or his mother—or the many others who are moved by a teenage boy's love for his mother. Such a grade would seem downright silly. Real writing goes somewhere and travels best when it is not weighed down by outside assessment.

Keri LaSalla, an eighth grader, wrote a poem because of a poem, an extended metaphor, that I wrote as a gift to my son, Brian. She then wrote a reflection on her poem.

Chanel

She would sit on the couch as Daddy arrived,
And peek her little head over the window and quickly scatter
off.
She always waited by the dinner table and licked up all
The dropped crumbs we had left.
She was there when we walked in the door from school,
barking so loud,
and wagging her tail brought a smile to our faces every time.
I told her what had happened in school that day and she
would sit there
and bark and sigh.
We hated to leave her alone, no one to bark at, or no one to
play with
All alone in the wall's shadow.
When we would arrive home from our absence, she was there
to bark and greet us at the door.
As our family gathered around the television,
She was there to lie with us and begged to be petted.
She hated to go out in the rain and get wet.
As she approached the door, we wiped her paws clean.
When her nose was cold and runny, we gave her extra love.
As she grew old, it became too late.
We still have her, but in our hearts.
We love you, Chanel, and we never got to say good-bye.

Reflection on "Chanel"

"Chanel" started out as an idea that came from my English teacher. Mr. Mahoney gave his son a beautiful poem for Christmas the past year. I got the idea to give my mother a poem about my dog, Chanel (pronounced like the perfume, Chanel #5), who had just passed away. I was sitting at the computer in Room 10 and I started to think of her actions and came up with the poem.

Mr. Mahoney helped me change it to make it more tasteful. His experience with English and my dog, together we became a team. Mr. Mahoney was pleased to help me to get this done in time for her birthday. I had exactly two days to finish this. On the first day, I completed the typing. That night, my grandma brought me to Genovese for a frame. The next day I cut it and framed it. That night my mother received it.

She loved it and was very happy. She started to cry, which made me cry. This became very important to me and I wanted to include it in my portfolio. I grew up with Chanel and she was my cheer-er-upper when I was down. My K-9 when I was scared and, most importantly, my best friend.

Keri wrote two other pieces that she also gave as gifts, a poem called "Godmother" that she sent to both her godmothers, who had moved to New Hampshire, and a short poem called "My Dearest Mother," which she gave to her mother for Mother's Day. Keri is typical of many of the eighth graders who found writing about people and giving their work as gifts to be a useful act for themselves and something to be cherished by those who received them. Her mother dropped Keri's portfolio off on the last date. She had put a sticky note on the back cover:

Dear Mr. Mahoney,
I am bringing this in for Keri—
Please let me know when we can pick it up.
I want to save it—forever.
Thanks,
Donna LaSalla

At the 1995 NCTE conference in San Diego, Nancie Atwell shared a poem that she wrote as a gift for her daughter, Anne, on her ninth birthday. Nancie's eighth-grade class had been studying the work of William Carlos Williams and his treatment of rituals, causing her to think about the rituals of her own life with Anne. Nancie wanted to show students how voices from the past can reverberate and how a parent and a child might say similar things, decades apart. This repetition of voices captured for her the way she taught her daughter how to ride a bike, using words very similar to those her own mother had used when she helped Nancie learn to ride. Nancie wanted to use these words as a prism for celebrating Anne's birthday through a poem about this ritual and Anne's growing up.

I typed out the poem to show my students not only how words can reverberate, but also how they can be used as gifts. I had been trying to write a poem about my then two-year-old grandson, Ryan. Because my son Tim and his wife, Debbie, live only ten minutes away, Ryan often comes to visit. We live a short distance from the Long Island Railroad tracks. The train comes with great regularity, blowing its whistle in both directions on its approach to a crossing spot very close to us. At the sound of that whistle, Ryan would always come running to me to be picked up to see the passing train. I would press him to my cheek and whisper things about the train. As often as not, though, we would miss the train because we heard the whistle too late and struggled to open the front door for our view. I thought of this idea of missing the train as a metaphor for missed opportunities and for my desire to capture each precious moment with Ryan. I wrote a poem about this ritual in my writer's notebook, calling it "Missed It."

I had an idea to give this poem to Ryan as a Christmas present, but I wanted some feedback first. I read it to my students and they told me what was clear and what wasn't. They didn't like the title because it sounded too sad. I remembered the title of Nancie Atwell's poem, how it indicated her daughter's age and the birthday gift. I decided to do the same for Ryan. The poem did not become a Christmas present because I ran out of time trying to find a photo of the two of us, me holding him, our eyes focused on the train. I asked Debbie to take a picture of Ryan and me at our front door, then I placed the picture in an oval I'd cut in the center of the paper. This time I called the poem "For Ryan, On His Third Birthday." I bought a frame for it and wrapped it up for his birthday in late May. The present initially made a bigger hit with the adults than with Ryan, but Tim hung the poem in Ryan's room over his bed. For a long time, Ryan asked his father to read the poem each morning when he woke up.

For Ryan, On His Third Birthday

It is late October and the leaves still block
our view through the front door
of the train that we raced to see
as it disappeared into the underbrush
behind the houses across the street.

I hold you at my chest as your wrap your arms
against my neck and your legs against my waist
and we look.
We have missed the train—
Again.

I lean my face into your soft, luscious cheeks
and whisper, "We missed it,"
but you don't frown at this lost chance.
I say to you, "There it goes, to-New-York . . ."
and pause for your well-rehearsed, whispered response,
"City," as you lean your cheek closer to mine.
Just minutes ago, as the train passed in the opposite direction,
and we made the sighting, I had said, "Going-to-St.-James . . ."
and you had chimed in as reverently, "Station."
I was thinking of how delicious the moment was and
the sad passing of these days
when I would not be able to press my cheek to yours
anymore at passing trains.

I whisper to you each time we miss the train
that we will get it next time
but that's no concern
since we've come to experience many aborted sightings
in the past twelve months.

It is no worry for me either
because you always come toward me
in sudden exultation, eyes gleaming,
stretching your arms at me to pick you up
and race you to our front door.

Catch it or miss, it does not seem to matter—
There'll be other whistles and other trains soon,
but right now, cheek to cheek,
I hold you tight and we head back down the short hall
To the kitchen
and your present life.
Yet I go slower than I might
because I wonder how often
I'll get to do this again.

I showed a copy of the poem and the picture to my classes, so they could see how I got a title after a long time. Jessica Ott decided to use Atwell's reverberating words and my poem to Ryan in writing about her aunt and uncle, part of her large extended family that had been left behind three thousand miles away. Jessica wanted to include an insight into life, the way Nancie's poem asks about the difficulties for parents in holding on and letting go and the nature of that struggle. The end of Jessica's poem states the importance of family as our greatest teacher.

To Denis and Andrea With Love

With open, outstretched arms,
And sparkling grins, I was always welcomed.
You spent endless hours
Playing,
    Talking,
        Listening.
Special occasions you were
At my side brightening
My day with words of
Encouragement.
Holidays were made
Extra special with
Your presence.
You included me in
Your family with
Love and generosity.
Although there are
Many geographical miles
Between us,
Thoughts of you are always near.

As each year passes,
I realize how much
You mean to me and
I know that I was
Always loved.

As you begin a
Family of your own,
I will imitate all you
Have done for me.
Although the relationship
Is not the same, I
Will always invite your
Daughters to be a great
Part of my life.
I will spend endless hours
Playing,
      Talking,
            Listening.
I will rejoice with them
In their accomplishments and
Help to wipe their tears.
They will always be welcomed
With love and generosity.
As the years go by, I will
Watch them grow into
Special people just like you.
I will follow your example
And show them that they will
Always be loved.

Family is your best friends.
Endless love and caring
Will be a part of
Our lives for
Generations to come because
Example is our greatest teacher.

SAYING THANK YOU

I heard about teachers who composed real pieces of writing in front of their students on overhead transparencies, so I decided to try "writing off the top of my head." The writing I had to do was a thank-you note for gifts I'd been given in appreciation for my coaching the girls' JV soccer program. I explained to my students that since the soccer season had ended, I had no choice but write a note to each of the eighteen girls on the team and send it to their homes. I began by writing some of these notes on a transparency to show my students how I would solve the problem of what to say after "Thank you very much for the wonderful gift." I also wanted to show them how to avoid sending a form letter by personalizing the message with a few comments about the person receiving the note.

I discovered during these discussions that students rarely wrote thank-you notes for gifts received on birthdays and other occasions. Most of the time, they picked up the phone and called the grandparent or relative to say thank you. I tried to convince them how much more enjoyable it would be if that same grandparent went to the mailbox and found a personal note, written in the child's own hand, addressed to the grandparent. I asked them to imagine the person standing at the mailbox, opening the letter at the curb, taking the time to read the note, and smiling, particularly if it was well written. The recipient might even read the note several times, perhaps even save it because it was so thoughtful. I pointed out how a phone call cannot be saved or displayed on a bulletin board or placed in the center of a table the way a nice card can.

We discussed what a nice card would look and sound like. During the first few minutes of each class that I taught that day, I showed students what I had written to that point and then wrote another few lines. By the end of the day, I had finished the letter. I showed the results to the classes next day. I explained how I was torn between using my own handwriting and using a very nice italic font on the computer and printing out the work on nice stationery. I showed them blank note cards I'd bought and explained how I planned to print out notes that I could attach inside the note cards. I would then personalize my opening and closing comments to each girl and could still use the same little story to each one about how I used the gift and how I appreciated their sentiments.

I made transparencies of a couple of different notes and showed how I individualized the messages to fit each girl. I then showed the students a few of the actual cards, the envelopes they went in, and the way I addressed them and put stamps on them. By the time I was finished, I had shown the students my composing process of crossing out and revising, and I had given them an example of real writing. All of this took three minilessons of about ten minutes each, so students still had plenty of time to continue working on their own writing projects while they learned about writing notes.

Later in the year, one of our English teachers, Marsha Green, was killed in a car accident on the way to school, leaving behind her husband, Jeff, and their daughter, Shaunna. A majority of the students in the school knew Marsha, so I decided to help them express their sympathy and condolences to Shaunna and Jeff by writing a condolence card in the same way that I had done for the thank-you cards. I invited students to do the same, inserting their special memories of their former teacher. I explained that such a card would probably bring comfort to Jeff and Shaunna when they read how the students remembered Mrs. Green. I gave students the home address so that they could mail their notes to the family. Some students asked for a writing conference to have me review what they had written, but most sent their notes on their own, just taking a cue from the tone and length of my note. When I visited the home a few days later, Jeff and Shaunna said how much they appreciated the outpouring of emotion from all of the students. This was another case of students using their writing for a real audience and not for a grade or to satisfy an assignment from a teacher.

CONNECTING OTHER SUBJECTS, OTHER CLASSES

Sometimes students are so deeply involved in their work in English and other courses that the work merges. Kerri Bovich wrote a poem as a result of her study in social studies class about the history of Vietnam. As Kerri said in her reflection,

> I got the idea to write this poem from Mr. Mahoney. During one of his famous mini (maxi)-lessons, he suggested that we try to write a piece that was based on facts. At the time, this idea didn't really appeal to me, but when I began to run out of themes for my writing, I remembered his suggestion.
>
> I included this piece in my portfolio because I think it displays the variety of pieces and risks that I took as a writer this year. I didn't stick to the normal poems and prose pieces that I have always written. I was also very pleased with the outcome of the poem, because it accurately portrays the ideas I found in my research.

> **The Pride of Vietnam**
> Crescendos of chanting voices echo
> over the mountainous countryside,
> celebrating the freedom of the Dragon.
> In the fertile rice fields,
> the people remember the heritage of the molded fish hook.
> Stocks that once held screaming victims
> have been cracked open, revealing a battling nation.
> The hill people stream from the deltas,
> fighting the wars for justice and civilization.
> A continuing, undying struggle for independence
> once more rocks the ancient land of South-east Asia.
> O, great Dragon,
> do not forget the culture of the Moi,
> of the Red River Valley.
> Do not let your peasants turn into
> soldiers in the face of another enemy.
> Continue your southward march,
> crying your unified battle cry.

The southern radicals,
in the twilight of socialism,
spill out of the embattled countryside.
A new Vietnam peers out of the guerilla traps,
as the mountains and rivers begin life anew.
Peace following the violet night,
regaining tranquility,
purging the shame of the mountain people.

Kerri's poem and reflection emphasize the ideas of ownership and risk-taking. Students must be given the opportunity to experiment with books they select and topics they choose to write about without the fear of some terrible consequence if the effort doesn't work out as planned. If they start a piece of writing that doesn't seem to be going well after a while, they must be able to put it aside for a period of time or abandon it completely. When students are given the opportunity to discover things for themselves, they will continue to surprise and astound their teachers. They will also find, as Kerri did, that the results are pleasing to them as well. Their words will seem like magic.

6 | MY READING CLASSROOM

A book should serve as an axe for the frozen sea within us.

Franz Kafka

A humorous definition of school says it is a place where young people come to watch old people work. If students are to become readers, they need practice reading, not sitting in class as their teacher discusses a book. After all, in an effective physical education class, students play the games or do the activities; they don't stand and listen to the teacher talk about a sport. The same is true of an art class or computer class: Students learn by doing. In English classes, which have so often been dominated by talking about texts, students need to spend more time reading.

Teachers have always been concerned about getting more students to read. But never before have so many students, including some of the best ones, been so turned off to books. During an SAT class this past spring, one of the students mentioned having a test on *Huckleberry Finn* the next day. "Oh, I hated that book," said Joel. "It was so boring that I stopped after forty pages."

"I never read it either," Meg said. "It seemed so dumb, about this kid who runs away on the river with a runaway slave. I couldn't even understand what he was saying half the time."

"Did any of you guys read *Ethan Frome*?" Mark asked. "That was the worst. Talk about dumb. Nothing ever happens. I read the first chapter and the last and then I got the *Cliff's Notes*."

"Wait a minute, folks," I jumped in. "Don't you read any of the works you're assigned?"

"I hate reading," said Jamie. "It's so boring."

"Hardly anyone in my class reads the books," Joel said. "The teacher reads some of it in class and she discusses it and goes over each chapter. Then we have the test. You don't really have to read to get a good grade."

My mouth hung wide open. "I can't believe this. How do you expect to do well in college? Here you are, taking up your good time in this SAT course and your parents are spending good money. Don't you realize that reading is everything in college? That half of the verbal part of the SAT is reading?"

"I used to like to read when I was little," Meg said. "I stopped in elementary school. My mother used to get me all kinds of books when I was little. I hate to read now. I just can't get into books right now."

Mark chimed in, "Only about a third of the kids in my 11 Honors class actually read the books, unless we read them in class, the way we did with *The Crucible* and now *Inherit the Wind*."

How could English teachers have allowed so many students to slip into their present state of apathy about reading? Even more important, how can we recover? How can we cultivate the passion to be transported to other worlds and to learn new things about the world? How can we get students to love to read the way we do? One way is the reading workshop, the other side of the writing workshop.

PRINCIPLES OF THE READING WORKSHOP

The principles of Jerry's and my reading workshop are the same as those for the writing workshop: time, ownership, and response. The classroom structure is based on how readers outside of school settings interact with and treat each other. I discovered that if I treated students as real readers, they would begin to do the same with me and with classmates. As we built up a trust for each other, we began to have some wonderful experiences. For some, this relationship came quickly, but for others, it took some time and much effort. From my observations and my professional reading on the subject, I began to develop certain principles.

Genuine readers respect the tastes and reading choices of others. They do not condemn books chosen by others as lowly or inferior, and they recognize that readers have a range of tastes, some of which change as they grow and move through reading experiences. What appears to be of great interest to a reader at one time may be just a passing fancy. Real readers recognize the existence of these changing interests and allow their friends the freedom to read widely. In other words, readers believe in the right to select their own books and to retain that right throughout their relationship. That is, they believe in *ownership*.

At the same time that readers respect differences, they look for similar interests in other readers because they want to talk about their reading. They want someone to agree or disagree with their interpretations and to share their emotional reactions to books. Readers are alone in the solitary act of reading. From time to time, they want someone to discuss their joys and sorrows with. They want *response*. No matter how much a reader has read, he or she is usually willing to discuss books with a fellow reader. Readers need not have read the same book to be able to have a conversation about books; they can rely on past books to sustain the conversation and to relate current reading to past reading.

When readers find others whom they trust and who give genuine responses, they sometimes seek advice about their new reading choices. They find that understanding each other's reading tastes encourages them to recommend books and seek recommendations. Most of us choose a book because someone we respect has suggested we read it, or because we want to have a reading experience that's similar to someone else's. At this stage, sharing our reading influences the choices of others, and we come to rely on each other's recommendations.

Readers want and need *time*. English teachers who have the luxury of summers off often describe those breaks as a time when they indulge themselves with all kinds of books because they finally have the time. Ask many adults about their reading habits and they will say that if they had more time, they would read more. Take away time from an already busy schedule and for most people, reading will end. All readers recognize that if given more time, they would use some of it for reading.

I took the principles of respect for individual tastes, need for response, and desire for more time and found that they worked my English classroom. It took constant reminders of these "real reader" principles, but I was able to develop some of this respect and enthusiasm for readers and books in my students. In time, it changed my life as well as the lives of my students.

STRUCTURE OF THE READING WORKSHOP

I used to designate Thursday and Friday for reading workshop. The idea behind reading at the end of the week was that as the weekend approached, students who were fully engaged in their work might be more inclined to continue reading on Saturday and Sunday than they would to continue writing. I saw the book as more portable and reading more flexible than the act of writing was. Students could more easily start and stop their reading than they could their writing.

In time, I noticed that my 11 Honors students would be more insistent, in their own quiet ways, on staying with a book or continuing with their writing when the schedule called for the opposite. Some, I discovered, could write in a setting that had noise and background chatter, but could not read in such a setting. Others could read through anything but needed their own computer or the complete silence of their own room to write. Who was I to dictate how they worked best when I knew that I could write in almost any kind of noise but couldn't read three sentences in a row without having to go back and reread when I was in a crowded room? For the most part, I allowed students to choose what work they would do in school and at home during the independent working time of each class. After I stopped designating certain days as being for only reading or writing, I told them that "I had lost control of the class" when the reality was that I was beginning to recognize learning styles and honor them. I began to allow students in my other classes to make their own decisions, though some needed more structure and guidance in choosing what to work on than my 11 Honors students did.

By the second year, I no longer differentiated reading days from writing days in any of my classes. Before that happened, however, on reading days I would give a five- to ten-minute reading lesson, followed by independent work. On writing days, I would give a minilesson on a writing topic. In time, these lessons seemed to blend together and I just gave minilessons on things that my students needed or might find useful at the time.

REQUIREMENTS FOR READING

I spoke with my students about how much reading they should be doing each day and each week. We agreed that about twelve to fifteen pages read a day between home and school was a reasonable request, and would amount to approximately one hundred pages a week and one thousand pages in a marking period. While strictly adhering to this figure would result in students playing a "numbers game" by trying to figure out ways to beat the system, we agreed that sometimes a student might be reading a particularly dense book and might not make the quota. Conversely, a student could choose books that were quick to read and not fulfill the spirit of our agreement. Setting a flexible target allowed students to recognize that they needed to budget their time to allow for reading but that they could also read in binges as their schedules permitted.

TEACHING SKILLS: IMPROVING SPEED

The first several weeks of school each year are crucial for establishing routines and creating an understanding of our approach to reading and writing for the rest of the year. My minilessons are devoted to how students can get things done, such as handing in literary letters, photocopying passages, holding writing conferences, taking "status of the class reports," and other procedures. By the fourth or fifth day, I give a lesson in improving student's speed in reading. Most students rate themselves as slow readers whether they are in advanced, regular, or remedial classes. They have either developed their reading speed by reading along with a teacher or student in class, or are plodding along with word-by-word reading. However, no matter what grade or level, when I ask students how many words a minute they read, hardly anyone has any idea.

To help students learn about reading speed, I photocopy a six- or seven-page short story from a young adult (YA) collection. I draw two lines down the first two pages, dividing the page into thirds, and number every five lines of the text. I make enough copies for a class set and hand them out. I tell students that we will be finding out how fast they read. To start, they should read for one minute at their normal rate. I start and stop them after sixty seconds and then ask them to make a tiny dot at the spot they reached when I told them to stop. I show them how to get an average number of words on each line by getting an average for the first five lines. Then I have them count the number of lines they read in the one-minute time period by multiplying the average number of words on a line by the number of lines they have read. Most students read 200–250 words per minute (WPM) in their first try, but there are often students who read fewer than 100 words.

Next I ask the students to hold their index finger in front of them and focus on the fingernail. I ask if they can see people to the left, right, and front without moving their focus away from the finger. They all admit that they can, so we establish the notion of peripheral vision. I point out that athletes use peripheral vision when competing and drivers use it to detect possible danger. I then stand up in front of the room and speak as if I am reading one slow word at a time, moving my finger across an imaginary page in front of me. When I come to the end of a line, I pause slightly, then jump down to the next line on the left. As I continue, I go back and repeat some words or phrases once or twice before I go on. I ask the class what I am doing and they always say that I'm going back to check a word I didn't understand. We call this action a *regression*.

I ask how many of them have watched MTV and what is happening on the screen. They point out that lots of images flash quickly before their eyes and then are gone. I ask if they are able to bring specific images back for another look. Usually they can't, but they understand the idea of the images. I tell them that that is exactly what they need to do when reading—to move through the words the way they move through music images, not going back to words they thought they missed but really didn't, words that they don't need as much as they think. I pantomime a story about how President Kennedy used to read several newspapers each morning to become aware of events in the world. I move my hand back and forth quickly over an imaginary newspaper like the arm and needle on a lie detector machine, moving down the newspaper rapidly and going to the next column.

On the chalkboard I draw a page of a book with two vertical lines dividing the page into three columns of text. I place my index finger on the first vertical line, just below the first line of text, and say that I am going to move my finger to the second vertical line every time that I say the word "move." I then start, moving my finger in a quick, smooth manner to the right and then down to the next line as I call out, "move, move, move, move, move, move," for several lines of text. I then ask the students to take the story they just read and practice moving their finger with their eyes at the same time that I say "move." We practice this for a minute or two, then I tell them to start at the beginning of the story and pace themselves for one minute. I do the pacing for about ten seconds, making my voice softer until only the students are doing the pacing. At the end of one minute, they put a dot at the point they read to. The students always begin to buzz about how they increased—even doubled—the ground they covered. We calculate their WPM and compare results. Some students say that they may not have understood what they read or everything that was there. I agree, but say that they've got to learn to speed up considerably before they can drop back down a little to a more comfortable speed. I compare this to needing to go faster to pass a slow-moving vehicle on a hill, then backing down to a more reasonable speed that will still keep you ahead of the other cars.

We practice a few more times with the story, each time calculating their WPM, which usually continues to increase. Then I ask them to try for three minutes. By this time, they can quickly figure out how many words they read in three minutes. They learn how to continue reading at a pace that exceeds their initial rate. I ask them to practice this at home in their selected book, and even to try to teach this to someone at home.

When the students come in the next day, I ask them what page they got to in their novel and how the practice with speeding up went. Most say that it was a big help. I make sure to practice this several times in the next ten school days to reinforce and solidify the skill. Often near the end of class on Friday I ask them to take out their novel and practice for a few minutes. I find this is a good way to get students connected to their books as the weekend approaches and they need the freshness of the story to entice them to read on Saturday or Sunday. One point I make all the time is that some texts are easier to read quickly, while others require a slower pace. A love letter, for example, may not be the most appropriate text for speed-reading, while a familiar story might be read rapidly. The point is not to race through texts, but also not to read so deliberately that it is like listening to a slow, monotonous speaker who causes the mind to wander. Comprehension actually increases when you pick up the pace and don't plod through the material. In time, most students agree that they have become much better readers.

TAKING READING RISKS

One way to evaluate students' growth in reading is to have them take reading risks, to move out of their reading comfort zone. When I asked one class what "moving out of one's comfort zone" meant, a bright girl named Adrienne gave this explanation: "If you liked reading in a chair where you are comfortable, you should get up and move to a different chair where you are not so much at ease." I thought at the time that she had completely misunderstood the idea, but years later, when she was once again in my class as a senior, I realized she had given me an analogy, not an explanation. I want students to move into new reading experiences rather than staying with the same author or genre endlessly. Sometimes they need a nudge from me to get them out of the comfort zone and to stretch themselves. If students are in the mystery genre and stuck with R. L. Stine, I might move them to Caroline B. Cooney, Mary Higgins Clark, Agatha Christie, or Sir Arthur Conan Doyle. I do this for all sorts of readers, moving them from easier books to books they might not readily find if they stayed in the same circles. The secret is not to demean their reading choices, but to broaden their horizons. Sometimes I write a few sentences at the end of a letter to a student, suggesting some other books in that category and giving a the student a choice of things to read.

CLASSROOM LIBRARIES

I cannot overstate the value of having a classroom library. It is crucial to be able to show students books to look over and talk about before they choose one or two to take back to their desk. It is also important for me to know the books and to know my students. Over time, we learn each other's preferences and can make recommendations. It is not unusual for me to read a book because one of my students liked it. For example, John O'Neil, a senior in my 12 Skills class, recommended *Where the Red Fern Grows*. Whenever I think of that book, I remember how John cried at the end of the book—a book he chose to read simply because it was on one of the bookshelves in the room. Many honors students, most of whom have greater access to books at home and from bookstores than other students do, select books that they have seen for a while on the bookshelves and are intrigued enough to pick up just after finishing another book. Many students have a habit of lining up books for their future reading, like planes on the runway awaiting takeoff.

Jerry and I order three or four copies of books to be distributed between classrooms. We choose YA books and best-sellers including Gary Paulsen, Chris Crutcher, and S. E. Hinton titles, or best-sellers for adults, such as *A Prayer for Owen Meany; Under the Eye of the Clock; The Shipping News;* and *Like Water for Chocolate*. When students have choices and are given access to treasures, they begin to anticipate reading many books and don't see each book as just another requirement to complete and be tested on. They find themselves in a reading mode. When we began our reading workshop approach, the high school library became a popular place and the librarian and the aides reported a dramatic, almost epidemic, increase in the number of books students were checking out. It took several years for this reading frenzy to seem natural.

KEEPING TRACK OF BOOKS READ

At the start of the year, I hand out a reading log sheet that students tape onto the inside back cover of their literature logs. They use this sheet to record the title, date completed, author, and number of pages of the books they read. In addition, they rate each book according to its degree of difficulty and indicate their enjoyment on a scale of 1 to 5. They also write a word or phrase of description. Looking at these reading logs helps me to know quickly what each student has read and what titles might be appropriate recommendations. Each sheet has space for twenty-three titles. When students fill up one sheet, they tape in a second or a third, as needed. As students began to keep track of their reading this way, I decided to do the same. Over the years I have read hundreds of books, most of which I would never have read because I had always been too busy reading and rereading the few books that I taught each year. Much to my chagrin, I had become an expert on a handful of books, but I'd stopped reading new titles. My reading life was bankrupt. As soon as I threw off the mantle of being the expert on select books, my life became much richer.

WHAT ABOUT WHOLE-CLASS READINGS?

I did not abandon reading books together as a class. I just don't do quite as many novels, and I don't use novels for nearly as long and as extensively as I had in the past. My 11 Honors class might read *To Kill a Mockingbird, Ethan Frome, The Catcher in the Rye, Huck Finn, The Great Gatsby*, and *The Crucible*. My ninth-grade class might read *The Pearl, Of Mice and Men, Romeo and Juliet,* some mythology, and another work or two. In reading workshop I tell students far in advance when we will be reading a novel as a class. For example, I'll hand out copies of *To Kill a Mockingbird* and after briefly introducing the book and doing a reading aloud, I'll ask students to read the first section, which is about 119 pages, by a specific date and write at least one letter about the novel. Sometimes I devote a few minutes in class to highlighting critical interpretations. I might point out the metaphor of the mad dog in the novel so students can look for it in their reading. I introduce themes, such as the idea of maturation and loss of innocence, that might be worth discussing with the whole class.

CLASSROOM DISCUSSION

On the date that all were to have read the first section, students moved into groups of four or five, determined ahead of time, and discussed things they noticed in the novel or were confused by. Most groups had little trouble with such discussion because they had been writing letters about the things that struck them in their reading. Their roles in the groups were based on the Patrick X. Dias (1987) method: discussion leader, recorder, reporter to the larger forum known as a *plenary*, minority recorder, and minority reporter. (If there are only four students in a group, one student takes the last two roles.) The discussion leader got the members of the group to share equally, providing order and organization to the way students spoke. The recorder for each group kept notes of the big ideas that the group had come to consensus about. The reporter spoke for the group, using the recorder's notes, when the class came together as a plenary. The minority recorder kept track of ideas that were presented but not agreed upon by all members of the group, ensuring that ideas could be presented to the class for further consideration. The minority reporter spoke about these ideas.

While Dias used this system for poetry, I used it for the novels the class read as a group. Sometimes I began with a few questions the groups might consider if they ran out of ideas to talk about. They turned their desks so that the four group members faced each other, close enough to speak in low voices. As students began their discussion, I moved from group to group, listening and asking how some theories squared with others. As a gadfly, I might arrive at one group and announce that another group was discussing a topic, then ask this group if they agreed. As they began to respond to me, I would move to the next group, leaving the first to ponder the response with each other. I never gave my insights, though students in the beginning used to say, "Are you going to tell us what all of this *really* means?" The purpose of the group discussions was to allow students to work through their own meanings.

On the third day we held a plenary session in which the entire class sat in a full circle. Each group reported on one or two things they had reached consensus on. I stood behind the circle and wrote notes on the front board as they were reported. After we listened to each group, we started again with other issues and challenges, including ideas that had not been accepted for consensus by the small group. These minority ideas were then held up for the whole class to consider.

We set a date for the completion of the novel and a similar discussion in which we tied together some of the ideas from the first sessions with the later views. Sometimes I asked that one of the finished pieces of writing for the marking period be an analysis of one of the novel's themes.

LITERATURE CIRCLES AND DIALOGUE JOURNALS

I also used literature circles for whole-class reading of denser, richer texts such as *Romeo and Juliet*, *The Scarlet Letter*, and *The Great Gatsby*. Harvey Daniels' (1994) approach asks student to focus closely on the text, which makes dialogue journals particularly useful. Before meeting as a group, the students spend time reading the work and finding quotations or excerpts appropriate to the roles Daniels has developed. These roles ask students to focus on ways that good readers read. The Discussion Director makes up questions for the group to discuss. The Artist draws sketches of issues from the text. The Connector makes connections from his or her own life to the text. The Literary Luminary selects passages for the group to focus on more intently, perhaps to read aloud or to dramatize. As students read and plan for their roles, they copy excerpts into their literature logs, which will serve for a time as dialogue journals. They divide each page into two columns with a line. On the left, students write excerpts from the text. On the right, they write their interpretations of the excerpts, or connections they have made. They bring their dialogue journals to their literature circle groups and discuss what they have figured out about the novel. These groups might meet two days a week for three weeks, or each Wednesday for four or five weeks. At the end, we have a culminating activity such as a skit, a dramatization, a literary analysis, or some work of the students' choice. While we work on the book, students still read and write as they were doing before, but I require fewer literary letters from them. They might write two fewer literary letters and write four to six pages of entries in their dialogue journals instead of the usual ten letters a quarter.

If we didn't have a whole-class reading, I would ask students to read at least one book that students in traditional classrooms might read. I brought in one or two copies of all the books a particular grade level could choose from and asked the students to choose one. Some students formed their own literature circles for the book and exchanged literary letters. Others read the work on their own without a group structure. When we met for whole-class discussions, I asked questions such as "How did you know your main character was reliable or telling the truth?" In this case, we would be investigating narrative techniques and I could specify kinds of narration found in the different books. At other times I asked, "When did you first know that the author was doing more than simply telling a story, but was trying to craft it? What words or passages did the author use to make you notice this?" This was asking about foreshadowing, imagery, and symbolism—not to test students but to allow them to discuss how different authors used these techniques for effect. At still other times, we talked about pacing and reflective narrators. I asked if students could remember passages when the narrator slowed the story down and revealed something personal or interesting about herself or about what she thought of things not directly related to the plot.

In *Opening Texts*, Kathleen Dudden Andrasick (1990) presents many ways for students to comment on their texts, including writing the following:

- a description of the kind of reader the text appeals to
- what students didn't notice or record in a text
- oppositions to several quotations, reversing the meanings of the original
- a single word and the feeling from saying the word again and again
- a classification of several pages of initial dialogue entries, based on different categories
- questions to a series of entries in the journal.

In addition, I gave students these options:

- Connect the text to other books, films, and world events.
- Connect the text to your personal experiences.
- Make predictions.
- Look up vocabulary words and their origins, looking for lesser-known meanings.
- Discuss a literary element like theme, image, or setting.
- Discuss stylistic devices such as repetition, understatement, and irony.

This discussion centers on the idea that many students have been asked only to examine literature as artifacts, not produce it themselves. As a result, students are robbed of the joy of understanding and appreciating texts because they have never been asked to place themselves in the shoes of the author. Teaching reading sometimes includes demystifying literature and allowing students to learn through the lens of authorship. After writing honestly, they can begin to work on a metaphor or a symbol or a developing image and make themselves more aware that the work they are reading may have those same elements.

One way to get at some of these reading skills is to ask students how they know when a flashback is occurring or what gives them a clue about a developing symbol. Once students begin to volunteer their strategies and the class can talk about how something is done, some of the mystery disappears. I then ask them to find an example from the book we are reading together, or from one they have read on their own. As we cite examples, students get a little more comfortable. I show a couple of examples on an overhead. One is from the beginning of *Ethan Frome,* where Edith Wharton uses a series of dots to move the story back in time. Sometimes writers will insert extra space or lines to show a gap in time. Often we can see shifts in time in a new chapter without any physical hints. I tell students that they have to look for that possibility in each chapter, particularly if the author is in the habit of making shifts in time. I offer the example of *The Pilot's Wife,* by Anita Shreve. In this story about a wife whose husband, an airline pilot, has died in a plane crash, the plot jumps back and forth between developing news of the crash and life before the crash. When I read this novel, after a while I could anticipate that the chapters would alternate between past and present. I can then send students back to their own reading to look for this literary element and to report it to us or write about it in a literary letter.

I tell students about John Irving's novel *A Prayer for Owen Meany,* and about how Irving develops several symbols in it. I tell them about the armadillo and the dressmaker's dummy and how Irving dwells on them by describing them in detail and continuing to refer to them. I ask why a writer would want to spend all that time on an item if he didn't want the reader to notice it and to think about it in many ways. I then turn to the opening pages of *The Scarlet Letter* and the description of the rose bush. I pose the same question as I did for *Owen Meany*, and we begin to suggest possibilities of what the rose might stand for. Having been made conscious of this shrub at the start of the novel, we believe that we can pay attention whenever it comes up and ask ourselves if the developing symbol is playing out as we had predicted.

NEGOTIATING SYMBOLS AND DEVICES

Reflective Narrators

Another skill that's worth examining from a reading point of view is recognizing reflective narrators. Many of us read because we want to know what happens next. We read because the story is riveting and the turns of the plot drive us to read more. When we are more reflective about a book, we are intrigued by characters who are real and who show us aspects of themselves that are very like or very different from the way we are. We feel we know what well-developed characters think and how they feel. Inexperienced readers are often not aware of when and how characters come to life and why we can identify with them. I teach students to recognize this in their work by focusing first on their narrators.

I hand out a photocopied page from a YA novel by Isabelle Holland called *The Unfrightened Dark*. The page also explains that a reflective narrator is one who stops and thinks about things as they are happening in the story, or about things that have happened. This narrator lets the reader in on more than just the events by sharing inner thoughts that other characters in the story may not be aware of. Writers often use the reflective narrator to let us know what they consider moral or immoral, right or wrong.

After reviewing the idea of the reflective narrator, we read the first few sentences of the excerpt from *The Unfrightened Dark* and locate the first place where the narrator is not telling us about the ongoing events in the plot but is providing background information or telling us how she feels. The narrator, Jocelyn, a blind high school girl with a seeing-eye dog named Brace, tells us about her Aunt Marion. I ask students to locate the first place that reveals how Jocelyn feels. I then ask them to underline each additional reflection and to circle any place where the action of the plot continues. On this particular page, the plot does not advance, but Jocelyn fills in background information about her aunt: ". . . and she's known for her charitable works to the needy of the parish and the community. Yet—." After giving us this information, Jocelyn tells how she feels: "It's the 'yet' that's like a wall between us, keeping us from being friends." She continues to explain that the "yet" has to do with her aunt not liking Brace. As we discuss this, I ask students to find the next place in the text where Jocelyn reveals her feelings of joy, worry, suspicion, doubt, or hatred. As they locate these feelings, students begin to understand. Then I have them return to the books they are reading individually to look for examples of reflective narrators or places where the author has slowed the pace of the plot to provide some other kind of information. I suggest that they mark the spot in the book with a sticky note, or write the spot down on a separate sheet of paper. Near the end of the period, I ask students to report on what they found. This is a topic that they can write a literary letter about, explaining things that good readers often notice, such as focusing on style or the author's technique.

I want to stress the value of using a minilesson to teach a skill or concept that students can use in their ongoing reading. I want to contrast that short lesson with lessons that last days, even weeks, on a text such as a novel or a play, exploring all the traits, techniques, themes, and other rich material found in the work. With this approach, students will demonstrate more knowledge about the text and may even appreciate it, but they don't readily transfer that knowledge to the next book they read. For example, I do a lesson on tone using Salinger's *The Catcher in the Rye*. Readers over the years have had a variety of reactions to Holden Caulfield. Often students don't understand his language, so I do a lesson on tone using Holden's expressions. I ask students to find examples of the expressions he uses frequently, and I write about twenty-five of them on the blackboard. These include "I hate it when," "terrific," "old," "crummy old," "helluva," and "really killed me." We discover that Holden uses many of these expressions as exaggerations to emphasize a point. We also note that he lies a lot and even tells us "I'm a terrific liar," so we know we can't believe everything he says. We have to look at his actions more than at his words to see how he feels. We agree that Holden is a typical teenager who uses language to hide some of his feelings and to exaggerate others.

As a conclusion to the lesson, I ask students to write in their writer's notebooks about something that bothers them, using Holden's expressions to imitate his style of speaking and capture his tone. These are always great fun to write and students are willing to read them out loud. One result is that students recognize that a person's words don't always reveal how he feels. Many students who have misunderstood Holden and seen him as a jerk who can't or won't grow up begin to see that his caring actions speak much louder than his bragging words. That brief lesson seems to go further than spending many days analyzing and discussing the novel. Furthermore, using a lesson this quick means that I am not keeping students from doing what they should be doing in a reading class: reading.

Another way of teaching narrative point of view is to have students choose a character from a novel and write a story from that person's perspective, using either a first-person or a third-person narrator. Giving students the option to choose a character and a narrative point of view lets them puzzle out what they want to emphasize with their character and which point of view will be most effective. I give them a handout with three poems I've written (Figure 6–1). The first is a first-person account by Scout as she stands on the porch after taking Boo Radley home at the end of *To Kill a Mockingbird*. I tell students that I want to emphasize how Scout's view of the neighborhood has changed. I mention that in order to get this poem correct in my mind, I had to go back and reread the last few pages of the novel to get the details straight. In doing so, I discovered several things and also found the term "winking lights," which I used for my poem's title.

The second and third poems expand on *Ethan Frome*. The second is written from the point of view of Mattie Silver, who urges Ethan to take them downhill on a sled and end their lives by crashing into a big elm. I emphasize that I made up some of Mattie's words based on how I thought she was feeling at the time. The last poem presents a third-person view of Zeena as she lies in bed feeling mean-spirited toward Ethan and toward life. I show the students that I can express Zeena's thoughts by using the omniscient narrator, who knows what the character is thinking.

This exercise takes no more than twenty minutes, including students selecting a character and trying out the approach by writing a beginning. We finish up by having students read their initial efforts to a neighbor, then listening to a volunteer or two who is willing to read to the whole class. This is not an assignment. The purpose is to look at texts and to respond to them, even imitating them. If students want to work on this further that day, they

Winking Lights

We climbed up the porch steps,
Boo and I,
he cool and quiet,
me still shaking at the near murder that night
and for the new friend whose hand I held
and who whispered, "Will you take me home?"

He has gone inside for the night,
and, though I don't realize it,
I will never see him again.

I am somehow different now
as I stand on the Radley porch,
looking at the street lights winking
all the way into town,
a new angle at looking at my neighborhood,
Boo's sightlines for all those years.

At this moment I realize that Atticus was right,
that you never really know a man
until you stand in his shoes
and walk around in them.

All of this has made me think of Tom Robinson
In desperate flight,
and poor Mrs. Dubose,
fighting
to leave this life
free
and even Mr. Cunningham at the jail,
frightened by his own fears
but pinched by the words of a little girl.

I still say Jem's crooked left arm
began with the Ewells
and not with Dill's arrival, as Jem says.
Atticus, in his own wisdom
would say we were both right
but looking at it all still makes me very sad.

—J. Mahoney

A Plea for Life

Down, Ethan, take us down
and fetch that Elm
which you said you could get.
I am young and fresh
and do not want to turn shrewish
like Zeena with her false teeth
in the tumbler by the bed.
If I can't be your sparkling Mattie,
you must put out the lights for us.

That's it, Ethan!
We are almost there,
and in the next world,
we will love each other
tender, and loving, and soft.
I can feel it coming
swiftly.
Lift me up, O Elm!
I am here!

Mean Spirited

She feels mean
and aches all over, her teeth in a tumbler
by the bed
as she watches her husband
rise early, shave, apply his Sunday lotion.

Her eyes become slits,
seeing his quick step
to the morning below the ladder,
knowing that trouble
lurks around the corner
like a waiting cat.

"Be patient," she thinks;
"the time will come
for me to have my way
once more.
No young thing will light a fire
in our hearth."

FIGURE 6–1. *Three Poems by Jim Mahoney*

are free to do so. If they want to pick it up on another day they can, because the seeds of the work are present in their writer's notebook. If they don't want to do anything more with this exercise, they are free not to. Not making this a writing assignment frees me from having to put a grade on the work, from having to catch up students who were absent, and from having to make a particular "creative" type of activity fit all students. There are always some students who will develop this activity further, polishing it and handing it in as part of their quarterly writing portfolio.

Reading Strategies

Stories contain many things that confuse readers, including flashbacks, multiple narrators, and dense language such as that used in long descriptive passages. Most students fail to connect what we learn about characters through their words and actions and through what others say about them with the characters' motivation for their actions. Students don't seem to be able to say why characters behave the way they do. Beyond that, the biggest reading problem for most students is the hidden meanings in symbols and figurative language that their teachers talk about but that they never seem to get. As a result, the students feel frustrated and inadequate. Literature continues to remain a mystery to them, open only to their teachers to find the interpretation.

Many students are never asked or shown how to write a poem in high school. Many have no idea whether a poem has to use rhyme, or where to get ideas to write about. Having no idea what I was going to write about, I told my students that I was going to try to write a poem right before their eyes. I turned on the overhead and placed a blank transparency on the glass. I began to ask the students what they were thinking and feeling about writing a poem. As they volunteered ideas, often reluctantly, I wrote them down at the top of the transparency. They said they were struggling with college; had jobs, money, friends, and parents to worry about; didn't like writing; were drawn together in this class because of writing. Some said they were sick with allergies; others were tired or sleepy. Some students said they felt foolish being asked these questions. They were confused by the questions and didn't know where I was going with them. Their poetry experiences were weak, and they were hesitant.

With these comments visible to the students on the transparency, I told them I was going to try and write about this stuff but that I still didn't know where I was going. Since we were using the Seamus Heaney poem "Mother of the Groom," which begins "What she remembers," I started with that line but referred to myself and my own weak academic beginnings. I wrote, "What he remembers is his own poor work,/scribbled handwriting of a 3rd grade paper," and then I remembered how dumb I felt in some elementary classrooms. I continued on the third line: "how foolish he felt/sitting across from Mary F./who always got 100's and perfect papers." I told the class that I was identifying with their frustrations by relating my own struggle to succeed in school. I said that I didn't know where I was going next with this, but I might now address them in their own struggles.

I decided to repeat the first line, but changing it from "remembers" to "thinks" and later to "feels." I wrote: "What he feels is for his students/who struggle to write honestly/but hesitate to speak out/or pour out a line/from their hearts." I told the students that many of them had just started writing with some honesty, but that they hadn't yet reached the place that they can get to as writers. I told them I appreciated how far they'd come in their first prose attempts but that I knew from experience that they would go further.

Using the idea of *knowing*, I started my third stanza with the line "He knows that many have never/been asked to try,/or have been shown how,/had their little hands held,/like shoe tying, to make a poem." I asked the students what they thought I meant by "shoe tying." Someone said that teaching a kid to tie shoes means getting down and showing the kid. At that point, I went to a boy in the back and asked if I could tie his shoe in a demonstration. To do so, I had to get next to him in his position, then make the bows and tell the story of the two rabbit ears and how they get tied together. I said that writing a poem is the same process, just working on one little image at a time. If they were lucky, I said, a nice little comparison might pop into their heads the way shoe tying popped into mine. If it didn't, the poem would still be good but could be crafted later on. I told the students that I could do more with the poem, but that if I wrote honestly, I could make a great start.

Annotating a Text

Recently, a student asked what she could do about her inability to concentrate on what she was reading and to remember what she had read when she was finished. She admitted that she was not at all "a reader" and that she was having this problem with her other courses now that she was asked to do so much reading. I talked about several strategies and then I asked if she knew how to annotate her texts. Most students don't know how because most of the books they read are given to them by the school and are not to be written in. As a result, students never get into the habit of doing what their teachers have done in all the books that they teach: They summarize, underline, highlight, draw arrows, and put in stick notes and index cards. How different the page in the teacher's copy looks from the page in the student's! By annotating, the teacher actively makes meaning of the text, emphasizing the areas to talk about with students.

I ask students to read through with me a photocopied page or two of a text, underlining or putting a question mark next to anything that is not clear. I do the same, working on a transparency. After a few minutes, I ask the students to say what they have done. Then I show them the first paragraph or two that I have marked up. I show them a paraphrase written out in the margin and a circled phrase that I think might be important. Then I ask them to try paraphrasing the next paragraph. They compare notes with a classmate. We make predictions. I ask them to do the next paragraph, urging them to see if they notice a pattern of repeated or similar words and phrases. If they find any, they can mark them with an asterisk because such words are probably going to be important. We establish that anything with an asterisk is like a main idea in a nonfiction passage: It carries some additional weight.

After doing several paragraphs, I ask students to write in the margin at the bottom, "This passage is about [blank] but seems to be suggesting that [blank]." Next to the second blank they write a big question mark, because here they are taking a risk and they need to recognize that doing so is the best way to come up with their own interpretations. We discuss the literal events of the passage and the interpretations that follow from them. I repeat this lesson with poems, novels, and nonfiction pieces so students can practice annotating a text and making calculated guesses. I find that any time I can get students to make marks on the text, they come closer to owning that text, to making the meaning theirs.

Quick Conferences

Having students talk briefly but pointedly to a classmate or two during a reading lesson is crucial to good discussion. In the annotating lesson, after students have marked up a passage or made a prediction, many of them need to try out or to rehearse their findings with someone less intimidating than the teacher or the whole class. I ask them to turn to someone nearby. I don't say which way to turn. I say that if there is no one near or if everyone is already paired up, they should make a threesome. These quick conferences are an icebreaker for students who are shy or intimidated by others in class. Too often, teachers assume that all students know all other students. When opportunities to talk authentically are not given, especially in an English class, some students will go through an entire school day not having a single conversation. Turning and explaining something to a classmate is a way of melting some of the ice of being isolated from others and intimidated by texts. After two or three minutes of discussion, I ask a range of questions, from "What did you learn from the person you listened to" to "Who found that the other person had exactly what you had?" Now I can ask students to say what their neighbor had to say or how they compared in the same way with their neighbor. These quick conferences take time, but they are essential for getting all students involved and focused on the many ways to annotate a text.

Asking Students

I ask students every few weeks to write a note to me about what they are doing best on and what they would like me to cover or to teach them personally. They always remind me of some basic issues. I might write on the board, "You've accomplished a lot so far but what are you still dissatisfied with or want to know how to do?" This allows me to go back to something fundamental, perhaps repeating the lesson, and it gives me a sense of where the class is regarding their reading. If several students say that they want to know how to pick good excerpts for their literary letters, I can get a small group together and go over this. If a large number say this, I know that I need to make this a minilesson very soon. I always make a point of telling students the origin of a minilesson that was requested by one or more students.

Themes and Big Ideas

Students have trouble with selecting or recognizing themes. Usually they don't have enough reading experience to do this well, and often they don't get enough practice in it. Until eighth or ninth grade, most students are not intellectually developed enough to make generalizations about a piece of literature. I begin a discussion about themes by writing a term such as "loss of innocence" on the board and explaining it, then asking if they can recall a time when they suffered a disillusionment. I ask if they can remember a book or film in which a young character is bitterly disillusioned. They name YA books like *A Day No Pigs Would Die* and *The Chocolate War*, and even *To Kill a Mockingbird*. We decide that to have a loss of innocence, you must have a trusting character who doesn't know all there is to know about the world. I then mention a related theme, initiation, whereby a character becomes assimilated into the world of evil. Again, the students name books and films in which this happened.

I name "romance," "courage," and "alienation" as themes found in literature, and I ask the students to name others. They come up with terms like "loss of spirit," "enchantment" or "magic," "mystery," and "greed." I tell them that some of the terms refer to genres or types of literature, but that some are also general topics that writers treat. I ask for topics that a writer might focus on in a novel. The students mention AIDS, sex, drug and alcohol use, intolerance, racial bias, and the role of conscience. When they name books or films that deal with these topics, I ask them to decide if the author is praising or criticizing. For example, I ask if Harper Lee is suggesting that the treatment of Tom Robinson by the lynch mob is good or bad. I then put that negative view in a phrase: "the ugliness of racial intolerance." This gives the topic a face that student can recognize. I mention Fitzgerald's treatment of disillusionment related to the myth of the American dream.

In *Romeo and Juliet*, we can see the impetuousness of youth, but we can also see the stubbornness of people in control or the destructiveness of feuds. We can also view the play's theme as the power of young love or the fickleness of fate. The point is, literature can use many themes. Students need to feel comfortable suggesting and defending their own interpretations of possible themes. Given the hands-on reading workshop environment, students accept the power given to them and make great strides in their development as readers.

7 | LITERATURE AND LITERARY LETTERS

Read, read, read. Read everything—trash, classics, good and bad, and see how they do it. Just like a carpenter who works as an apprentice and studies at the mast. Read! You'll absorb it. Then write. If it's good, you'll find out. If it's not, throw it out the window.
William Faulkner

Do we teach reading or literature or, as Tom Romano (1995) calls it, LIT-RA-CHURE? Most English teachers learned by studying the great works and renowned authors. I'm not denying the value of reading those works and writers, but my teaching focus, even at the high school level, was on the act of reading and the benefits that accrue from it. I brought great works to my students' attention. However, my goal was not to make students little English teachers, engaged in the same kind of study that teachers did as undergraduate and graduate English majors. I had carried some of that philosophy into my early years of teaching. When I began to view things differently, I was no longer interested in testing students' knowledge about the great works or the lesser works. I wanted students to read books that made connections to their lives, to their larger worlds, and to the things they were learning in their other classes. When I took the capital L off *literature*, I was asking students to be readers and not students of literature. I also pushed individuals and whole classes to take risks with their reading, directing them into more challenging works when they were ready for the challenge.

YOUNG ADULT LITERATURE

A year ago I asked a group of student teachers at my Wednesday evening seminar at a local university to look at the copies of the young adult (YA) novels I had handed them, read each one for a minute or two, and then pass the book on and receive the next one. After ten minutes, I asked them to imagine that they had decided they wanted to teach one of these novels, and then to write the words they imagined their cooperating teachers would use to answer their request to do so. I had the students, one or two at a time, write these imagined statements on the board. Here's what they came up with:

"That's great! If you think you can use it, go for it. Let me know if I can be any help with this."

"That's trash and can be read in about twenty minutes!"

"We don't have time for that stuff."

"That's great! What exactly did you want to do with that book?"

"We only read books in the curriculum."

"Those are the books they can read on their own. We only read books that are considered classics."

"We don't deal with books like that. We only deal with high-quality works. These can be read anytime."

Now when I give a workshop, I show this list of responses to the teachers who attend and ask them four questions:

Which response most represents your reaction?

What response is least like yours?

What response best represents the power/decision-making force in your school?

What response might be missing, perhaps a response you'd make or like to see?

Most teachers say their own response is most like the first and fourth and that the persons making the decisions would say things like the remaining five comments. I am always disappointed by the missing response. I would love to hear a teacher say, "Oh, I hated that book because of [reason], but I loved her latest book about [subject]." Or, "I loved that book, but you should read his first one before making any final recommendation. That book captures the spirit even better." In other words, I'd love to see teachers respond reader-to-reader, rather than judge-to-jury. I'd like to see them show familiarity with YA books before they encourage or dismiss them.

My experience is that most teachers have not read very many YA books, and therefore make judgments on the basis of limited knowledge. Imagine your doctor dismissing a possible solution to your mysterious illness without having read all there is to read in the field. My sense is that we have many needy kids in our classrooms who hate reading and don't read, but we continue trying to cure them with the same remedies used in the past—difficult, unappetizing classics that depend on good teaching and high motivation to gain some success. Powerful coaxing does not substitute for changing the menu. It's reading and the love of reading that we want, not just reading "good stuff."

Since I turned over a large portion of the control of book choice to students and no longer had to spend hours reading new school texts each year, I've read hundreds of YA books at the same time that I was reading "grown-up" books. I have come to know with a degree of expertise all the books that Robert Cormier has written and all the works of Chris Crutcher, Gary Paulsen, Cynthia Voigt, Caroline B. Cooney, Jerry Spinelli, Walter Dean Meyers, S. E. Hinton, Paul Zindel, Katherine Paterson, Karen Hesse, Robert Lipsyte, and others.

I have also read a good selection of books by Christopher Pike and R. L. Stine. I've long maintained that Christopher Pike's characters seem not to take a moral stance on anything. Rarely if ever do his main characters think out loud about an intellectual or moral position related to the events of the story. In fact, many of his characters appear to be immoral or incapable of reflecting on their actions or those of another character. R. L. Stine, on the other hand, does not seem to have immoral characters, though he does present situations in which characters do bad things. Stine does not spend time on the internal lives of these characters, instead dwelling on plot and creating suspense and fear by making events unfold rapidly. I don't think these books should be banned or that students should be kept from reading them. But it is the job of a good teacher to raise questions about reflective characters who consider moral choices. Students can be asked to find evidence of such traits in their books. I've found that students, even those in high school, soon jump to more challenging books that speak to their own emotional and psychological concerns—the issues that most YA authors address.

Listen to Robert Cormier talk about his novels and you will realize that he is working with the idea of a conscience at work. Even though he opens *We All Fall Down* with a group of teenage boys not only wrecking a house, but desecrating it as well, the rest of the novel presents the agonized conscience of one of the boys as he deals with his acts and their consequences. We can see through Cormier's character a moral issue and how evil works within and on a person. Some of his books have been banned in schools, the most prominent being *The Chocolate War*, but his treatment of good and evil may be one of the most important qualities of a good English class. Where other than in stories can students examine these values, which are central to our society? Where else can students discover what happens to an individual when he commits an evil act? We shouldn't block or ban students from examining the acts of evil in a book because by examining such acts, we can help students understand themselves and the world that they're encountering in their reading. Teachers who say YA books should be read on students' own time are denying the opportunity to discuss the very books that students actually want to read—books that are not honored as authentic in the classroom.

It is a hard sell to get ninth graders to identify with Pip, Odysseus, Kino, or Lenny. It is much easier for them to identify with Ponyboy Curtis, Jerry Renault, and Dillon Hemingway. If students are given opportunities to connect with characters in YA literature throughout their adolescent development, they are much more likely to understand the protagonists in the other books typically taught in English. In other words, YA books should be honored alongside the books in the canon, not below them. Chris Crutcher has more than once told the story of the talk he gives to teenagers. After all the well-wishers depart, one girl hangs back to say to him quietly, "I read *Chinese Handcuffs* and I thought you knew me." This girl is saying not only that she connected deeply with the book, but also that she found in it a safe place where another character had the same horrible secret that she had. The last thing a wounded kid wants to do, Crutcher tells us, is reveal his secret to just anyone. Instead, he wants to be told, through the safety of a book, that he is not the only one who feels like this and that he is not crazy. Teachers who understand their students can direct them to the right books, the ones they just might need at that time.

Jonathan Kozol, in his opening banquet speech at the NCTE (National Conference of Teachers of English) conference in Nashville in 1998, spoke about how many good teachers there are who bless their students by their honest efforts every day. He says that it is the job of teachers to bless their students who come to school with hurts and needs, and that these teachers, by their kindness and wisdom, care for these children. In some cases, such teachers are the most caring adults kids may encounter all day. Teachers who give students books they need are, in Kozol's words, the real saviors.

Chinese Handcuffs, which deals with the sexual abuse of a high school student, need not be given to every student. The novel has many other issues and themes. However, if a book is powerful and other students learn that it is, they will recommend it to their friends. There will be more students accepting recommendations of books from their peers (when they have choices) than if they only hear the recommendations from the teacher.

LOTS OF BOOKS

I have found for myself that when I am surrounded by books to choose from, I will be reading my next book sooner than if I have to wait to go to a store or to the library. Jerry and I always ordered lots of books in quantities of two and threes for our classrooms, not all of them YA books. As I was reading and getting literary letters from my students about a book, I would often find myself wanting to read that book because of the student's recommendation. I selected *Ironweed, A Prayer for Owen Meany, Their Eyes Were Watching God,* and others because my students had told me about them. But the thing that also helped me make the selections was that the books were right at my fingertips, sitting there on the shelf for me to pick up and read. There is no substitute for availability, for having inventory on hand. To make books available in individual classrooms, Jerry and I, along with another teacher or two, would go through paperback book catalogs and select packages of books such as "Newbery Award Winners" and "Books About Outsiders." With twenty-four books in a package, we would order two sets of each package, and two or three packages. The cost would be about $700 for a classroom. This often included some individual titles that weren't included in the packages but that were worth getting a copy or two of.

I never wanted to order those fancy anthologies that cost over $50 each. For that, I could buy ten or twelve hardbound copies of YA books. What do I have against anthologies? Almost everything! In my first few years of teaching I loved an anthology, but in time I found that they contained far more selections than the students ever read. Getting students to bring the books to class and home was a major problem. Keeping students from writing in them was always an issue, as was replacing them when they were lost or damaged. These were just the pragmatic reasons that I faced as a young English department chairperson. The deeper issues did not present themselves to me until I began to see my students as real readers. They needed to read real books, not collections that had been anesthetized so that they appealed to committees on textbook adoption. I thought of how I prized reading in bed before I fell asleep each night and how, sometimes as I finished a book, maybe with tears in my eyes, I would press the book to my chest and feel close to the book and to the reading experience I had just completed. Try as I might, I couldn't imagine clutching a big anthology to my chest. There is something special about a reader and a book. I think this is what most of my students came to discover as well.

LITERATURE AS INERT OBJECTS

In an article called "Untold Stories: Culture As Activity" (2000), Bruce Pirie makes the case for seeing our culture as a combination of all the told and untold stories. He says that we have told many stories of our world as we've seen it, but that there are still many stories that have not yet been told about our past as well as about a future that has not yet happened. Pirie suggests that when we stop telling those stories, our culture dies. He is talking not only about recognizing that we all have stories we need to tell, but also about the way we treat the stories that have been collected into the body of literature that often serves as the English curriculum. He suggests that our job is more than transferring this culture to our students. If we see this body of literature as a kind of fixed and permanent form of art "to be carved up like food and served to our acolytes," we have missed the point. Pirie suggests that the body of literature is unfinished and it is there to be acted upon by new readers who create new stories as a result of the old ones. He cautions, "Once our stories become icons of greatness to be stored and admired as museum pieces, once we believe there are no more stories to tell, then our culture becomes dusty and dies."

Robert Scholes (1999) makes the same point as Pirie, saying that texts can't be treated as high culture to be interpreted and explained by high priests like Monsieur Swann in Marcel Proust's *Swann's Way*. Swann realizes sadly that his tastes are superior to those of the girl he loves, but he can't show her how the works he values would be interesting to her. Scholes suggests that works of literature are useful when seen as vehicles that allow readers to make meaning of their lives and their world.

At a 1992 NCTE convention, Nancie Atwell told the story of a field trip she and her students took to an art museum and of how the people in charge of the museum treated the students as potential threats not only to the art on display but to the adult visitors as well. They were warned about keeping a respectful distance. In response, Atwell sent the museum staff a letter and a copy of Richard Wilbur's poem "Museum Piece," reminding them that art is made *by* human beings *for* human beings.

The arts must be seen as alive, dynamic, and for the people—objects to be used in the creation of new art. If English teachers don't allow students to create new art through the things we teach, instead holding them to admiring and regurgitating symbol, theme, irony, and metaphor, our culture truly becomes "dusty and dies" for these students. Sensing these ideas and wishing to have my students become respectful readers on the journey of discovering and expanding their tastes, I set about giving up my power as keeper of the meanings of literature and allowed them to discover with me how wonderful our findings could be. I abandoned weeklong discussions of literary works, stopped using quizzes and tests "to keep students honest," and gave up control of what students would read. Instead, I gave them time to read, opportunities to select their own reading, and ways to provide responses to what they had read.

LITERARY LETTERS

Though there are many ways in which readers may get responses from their classmates and me, we agreed that writing the equivalent of a literary letter once a week to me or to peers would be the target. (This equivalent could be dialogue journal entries, book discussions, etc.) For approximately every hundred pages a student read, she would have some way of reflecting on the book and getting feedback. By the time the marking period ended, students would have ten letters. I asked that students write two letters to me and eight to their peers, and I gave them dates when they needed to give me a letter. I then posted these dates on the front bulletin board. I staggered the due dates over the marking period to ensure that I would not be swamped with letters and thus prevented from giving full, thoughtful responses to the ideas they had chosen to write about. I said that they could give me a letter at any time they wanted as long as it was before the due date. Even then, I hardly worried about a letter that was late a day or so, as long as the student explained the problem to me. In rare cases when I thought a student was trying to take advantage, I told the student that I would not give credit for a very late letter. Students accepted that as fair and never complained.

When students first began writing literary letters about their books, most seemed to be summarizing the plot or talking in generalities about things they liked or noticed. As I received more and more letters, I began to realize that I appreciated and understood more fully those letters that pinpointed specific issues, even quoting pages and lines from a book. I noticed that some students were actually copying out passages to illustrate their point. I showed in minilessons some of these more interesting letters and explained how students used the quotes to give the reader a sample of the reading.

We decided that a literary letter should usually have at least two quotes or excerpts from the text. I also showed sample letters that were *thorough, thoughtful,* and *truthful* (the three Ts)—three qualities of good letters. We discussed how such letters were fully developed with specific details, had good insights and not just plot summaries, and were honest in talking to the reader about the book and its issues. When we looked at the good letters, we noticed that most of them were about five hundred words or more in length, not counting the excerpts. We noticed too that letters with good responses were about two hundred words (a page or so) in length, but that they referred to some of the writer's specific comments with thoughtful statements. As a result of discussions with all my classes, we began to set some acceptable standards for literary letters and responses.

FINDING PASSAGES TO QUOTE

At first when I asked students to include excerpts in their literary letters, I used the word "quotes," asking students to include two quotes in each letter. To many, a book was just a collection of words and paragraphs, and picking quotes was like playing blindman's bluff, stabbing in the dark for something. When we read several pages of a novel or short story together, I showed the students lines that reminded me of events in my own life, incidents from other books I had read, or current conditions in the news. I showed them how I made connections between the text and the many aspects of my life. I asked them to do the same. I gave them prompts such as these:

> After I read the passage, I began to think of . . .
> I was confused by . . .
> I thought of the time . . .
> I could not believe . . .
> I loved the way . . .
> I felt . . .
> I was surprised . . .
> I noticed that the author . . .
> If I had been there, I . . .

I asked what each of these prompts had in common, and students noticed that they all had the word "I" in them. "Yes," I said, "and that's one difference between a literary letter and what some of you remember about book reports. I'm interested in what *you* think and feel about your book, and I don't want you to spend your time summarizing what the book was about. This is your gut level response to the work. It's first-draft, unrehearsed, reader-to-reader." I told them this did not mean that they were to write the letter sloppily or in a rushed way, but that they didn't have to have thesis statements, have the book and the characters all analyzed, or know all the symbols and themes. I told them that as they wrote more letters, they would begin to grow in sophistication and appreciation for the author's craft, but that wasn't the purpose of these letters. These letters were to tell a friendly fellow reader what a student thought as she read a book. I wrote on the blackboard, "A good literary letter tells us as much, if not more, about the reader as it does about the book."

Finding passages or excerpts was easier once we used the prompts. The students copied passages that sparked feelings including confusion, surprise, disgust, and pride. It was not enough simply to say, "the passage surprised me," and then quote the passage. It was important to say what the student had expected and what actually happened to cause the surprise, perhaps indicating what would have been done in that situation or what actually was done in a similar situation. In other words, the letter writer had to elaborate and give an insight into his or her thinking. Students soon learned that they might make a statement associated with a prompt, explain it a little, even give a sentence or two of plot explanation, then provide the excerpt and follow that up with several sentences explaining their personal connection to the passage.

PROVIDING THE QUOTES

To give the reader a good sampling of the book, students would sometimes select long passages, requiring meticulous copying from the book. Some discovered that photocopying a page from the book and then cutting out the passage was much easier than copying the passage by hand. Furthermore, some students were willing to go to the school library and spend ten cents a page for the copies. Others were not as willing or able to spend their money on things connected with school, so they struggled with the quotes and compromised themselves by writing very brief excerpts. I decided to give a few dollars in dimes to the librarian, who would then hand any student in my class a dime for the photocopy machine. Before I knew it, everyone in my classes was requesting dimes from the librarian. I had to take another approach.

Our principal, Dan Nolan, suggested I get a small copy machine for the classroom, using funds from the PTA. We agreed that this machine would be used only for literary letters and would be placed on a portable cart so that other teachers could also use it for their literary letters. We kept the cart in the back of my classroom, where I also placed a paper cutter, scissors, and tape. Students then had all the materials needed to copy passages, cut them out, and tape them into their letters. I almost immediately saw an increase in the depth and length of their literary letters because students were willing to select longer passages and specific things that they could respond to.

The final step was to compose letters to Mr. Nolan and to the PTA, thanking them for their help in allowing everyone to be more productive.

Some students will instinctively figure out things like responding and using excerpts, but these skills often remain mysteries to those who don't have certain instincts or environments. Teachers must unlock these secrets by showing students how to crack the code. To do so, we compared literary letters that had inviting openings with letters that were perfunctory and started right in on the book without paying any attention to the person receiving the letter. Students agreed that the letters they liked to receive were those that contained a personal reference or something shared with the writer. We referred to such letters as chatty and inviting, even gossipy. The students decided that bad letters were ones that were written the night before without a specific person in mind, and that had a name added the next day for the one who would receive the letter. We called these "form letters" or "junk mail" and discussed how they had such little personal value. Good letters had good openings, a friendly greeting, and some statements of mutual concern: the upcoming weekend, all the work students had, anxiety about the prom, or some other references. They also mentioned projects the reader was doing in the class and how he or she had chosen the current book. The writer might explain the setting for the letter: "I'm home sick with a bad cold." "I'm in the cafeteria right now and I'm writing with a mound of garbage piled in front of my literature log." "It's three in the morning and I couldn't sleep so I decided to come down to the living room and write you a letter. I didn't want to wake my sister by putting on the light in our room."

Some comments might be reserved for the end of the letter, such as an invitation to study together for the upcoming test, a lament about how fast the year was passing, or a wish that vacation time would come more quickly. The comment might also be a promise to read the recommended book next or to loan the reader the book as promised. Essentially, the good literary letter is a personal communication in written form, reader-to-reader.

SAMPLES LETTERS

Personal attention, care, and concern are qualities we appreciate in letters from our friends. In the introduction to a literary letter, Jeff addresses his good friend Liz with some personal notes about her team's upcoming cross-country meet.

Dear Liz,

As I sit here and write this on Halloween night, the eve of the County Championships, I cannot help but think of the feelings of anxiousness that you and the rest of your team must be experiencing, and the feelings of approaching freedom that I am feeling. For this reason (and the fact that I need more lit letters), I have decided to enlighten you with the best literary letter that my somewhat demented mind can afford.

As you may be aware, I am reading a book called *The Poe Reader*, by, you guessed it, the one and only Edgar Allan Poe. . .

Liz writes back warmly:

Dear Jeff,

Thanks for the letter. I always enjoy hearing from you. You're right, by the way. It was a good one. That was pretty interesting how Edgar Allan Poe was a poet and *then* a prose writer. His stories are fantastic! My favorite is "The Pit and the Pendulum." Remember when we read that in 8H grade with Mrs. Sommerstad?

I never read the poem "The Raven," but when I finish the book I am reading now, I'm going to definitely read it because you sure have gotten my curiosity up about the "Quoth the Raven, Nevermore" stuff. I just have to know what it's all about.

Kerri writes to her friend, Katy, thanking her for a book and referring to things that were brought up in class. She asks for her friend's interpretation.

Dear Katy,

First, I have to thank you very much for letting me borrow *The Hiding Place*. I loved this book the first time I read it and I loved it again. What Mr. Mahoney says is true; when you read a book for the second time, you pick out information that you missed the first time. It helps even more when there are highlighted paragraphs because they stand out, causing me to contemplate them more (and then I wonder what meaning they had for you).

Kerri remembers a book that I read and starts a conversation:

Dear Mr. Mahoney,

Hello. How are you doing? I have just finished reading *The Giver* by Lois Lowry. If I am not mistaken, I believe that you read this book before. How did you like it? Personally, I thought the book was great. Last semester I read *Brave New World* by Aldous Huxley and I loved that too. Many people told me *The Giver* was along those lines so I decided to give it a try.

The closings of letters can also be insightful and personal. In a long, beautifully detailed letter, Marissa talks about the deep impact that a novel had on her:

> I was so happy when Rocco realized he could do anything. Everybody can do anything. It annoys me so much when people say, "I can't do it!" I am a total hypocrite, though, because I say it all the time. My boyfriend is another story. He is so smart, has so much talent, but he wastes it all. It makes me so frustrated, so sad too.
>
> Well, I really enjoyed the book, especially the second time. I am sad, though, because I enjoyed this so much. I wish it wasn't over. I am going to go to the library and see if there are any other good books by Richard Price, the author of *Clockers*. Well, it was nice writing to you. Have a Merry Christmas!
>
> Love,
> Marissa

MY REPLIES

My responses to these letters are honest, personal, and supportive, traits that I've found are essential in establishing a good rapport with students. Here are the last three paragraphs of my response to Marissa:

> You're right about being able to do anything. As I'm entering my next phase of life (leaving teaching one of these next 1–3 years), I panic at what I'll do and whether I'll be any good at it. As much as I've loved teaching for 34 years, and in some ways don't want to stop, another part of me wants to do something totally different. Will I be any good at that? The unknown makes cowards of us all.
>
> By the way, I've always been struck at seeing bright girls having boyfriends whom they recognize as wasting their talents, etc., and still they go out with them. I don't know why but it always strikes me as strange. I always wanted to go out with a girl who wanted to do "big things" and make a difference in the world. Such a person helps to inspire the partner to be great as well. I think that's been one of my wife's many strengths.
>
> Anyway, thanks for a great letter. It inspired me to write a long response. So much to talk about.

Sometimes students want to begin a letter by talking about other work they're doing in class. Steve tells Jeff about his writing plans:

> Dear Jeff,
>
> Well, you may be surprised to see that this is my first literary letter of the new marking period. Just as you did last quarter, I am con-

centrating a great deal of time on my different writing pieces. But more than that, I've been writing a great deal of different things in my writer's notebook, a lot more than I usually do at the beginning of quarters. In fact, normally at the beginning of quarters, I spend a lot of time with my literary letters, but this quarter it has switched. I must be honest with you, however, and admit that I have not had a lot of time to read because of the great amount of school work that I have had. This fact also contributed to my lack of literary letters.

Well, enough of what I am *not* doing; on to the book . . . The novel that I am reading is entitled *The Education of Little Tree* by Forrest Carter, an American Indian who grew up and lived in New Mexico. The novel is supposedly an autobiographical account of his youth with his grandparents. I read this book in sixth grade and it was perhaps the only book that ever made me cry. It had been passed to me by my mom to whom it had been shown by my "grandma" in California. It is really the kind of book that you actually laugh and cry to in public, the kind that really moves you. I had often thought of rereading it, being that most of the things that you read and do that far back get lost in the file cabinets of the mind. But it wasn't until I was looking for a book for my younger brother Tom to read and giving him this, that my interest really spurred me to read it. His reaction to it was simply enough for me to pick it off the shelf for myself. When I found a newly printed hardcover edition at Borders, I decided to buy it and I have been reading it since. If I could recommend one book for you to read, this would be it. It is probably the most moving piece of literature that I have ever read.

Steve has endorsed and suggested a book for his good friend and reveals how deeply it has affected him. He reveals more about the book and provides passages from the novel for Jeff to sample. True to the spirit of Steve's letter, Jeff tells Steve about a time when he was touched by a book:

Well, as for your book, I know the feeling. I too cried once while reading a book. It was two years ago and the book was *The Runner* by Cynthia Voigt. I began reading it as per a recommendation by Liz. She said I would love it. I was skeptical because at the time I was in my "Stephen King or Bust" stage. One Saturday night at about 11:30, I began to read the book, thinking it would be a good way to get to sleep. Well, four and one half hours later, at about 4:15, I finally shut off my light, having finished the book, lying on a pillow soaked with my own tears. I had never been touched so by a book. It was then that I realized that there was so much more than words on paper in books. There was feeling, energy . . . life. So I know how you feel.

Jeff

In Jeff's reply, we sense far more than a book report between two eleventh-grade friends. Both have admitted crying over a book. In addition, Jeff tells of his doubts about a book recommendation from Liz, another good friend, but reveals that he tried the book anyway. Imagine how hard it is for students to trust teachers when they are even skeptical of friends' recommendations. Jeff is also able to recognize his own reading binges and refers to his obsession with books by Stephen King. When students have a wide range of reading experiences and individual choice, they soon begin to reflect on their reading experiences and talk about having developed some literary tastes and preferences.

WRITING LETTERS ABOUT STYLE

Sometimes I gave minilessons on styles that authors use and ask students to tell in their literary letters about specific techniques they notice in books. In a letter to me about *Ethan Frome*, Alan starts by discussing the picture on the front cover of the novel and then presents examples of style that contribute to the harsh setting of Starkfield.

Dear Mr. Mahoney,

I've zipped through a couple of short stories so far this quarter. I read *Old Man and the Sea* and have now finished *Ethan Frome*. It was a dramatic change of setting from the scorching Caribbean Sea to the frozen, snow-covered hills of Starkfield. There was also a sharp contrast between Hemingway's simple, yet effective descriptions of the sea to Wharton's more sophisticated and more complex sentences. However, both styles of writing served the purpose of the author to create captivating stories. I do feel that because Hemingway's story contains simple vocabulary, it could probably be read and enjoyed by a greater number of people at all age levels, as opposed to *Ethan Frome*, which would most likely appeal to only those who could read through the vocabulary and also relate to the love affairs of Ethan. In short, I don't think someone in the fifth grade, for example, would enjoy *Ethan Frome*, yet *The Old Man and the Sea* would probably be a big (or at least bigger) hit.

When I first looked at *Ethan Frome*, I found the picture on the cover very intriguing. As I read the story, different aspects of the painting took on even more significance. First of all, the picture set the scene for Edith Wharton to describe the winter landscape of Starkfield. Secondly, the drawing shows several sleighs occupied by people with simple external appearances. Although I got a general feel for the simplicity of the town, the picture doesn't tell anything about the lives of the people in the picture. It's as if each person has a hidden story that lies somewhere beneath the blanket of snow. Finally, each plot of land in the picture is divided by fences. These partitions seem to isolate the homes, just as the true story of Ethan Frome was isolated from the knowledge of the narrator. Even the path past the house on the top of the hill seems to lead off into the unknown, and the Frome household could be imagined to be on the other side of the hill, accessible only to those who would have to go out of the way to find information about the people who inhabit these isolated houses. Since I've talked about this picture for over a page now (originally notebook paper), and I just remembered that you have a different copy of the book, I decided I'd better put in a picture for easy reference—I guess this could be considered one of the "stranger" quotes to be found in a lit. log!

In fact, I feel that the setting is what makes *Ethan Frome* effective. Wharton goes to great lengths to make sure that Ethan's love for Mattie is the only warmth in a frigid, cold and bitter existence. It is this stark(field) contrast that makes the book a success. Whenever Wharton describes the landscape, cold adjectives are used, but when she describes Mattie she often uses "warm" adjectives. She also uses shades of gray, white and black when describing the land, yet uses brighter colors for descriptions of Mattie. Here are a couple of my favorite examples which illustrate this point. Cold images are underlined, while warm images are italicized.

COLD EXAMPLE:

The village lay under two feet of snow, with drifts at the windy corners. In a sky of iron the points of the Dipper <u>hung like icicles</u> and Orion flashed his <u>cold</u> fires. The moon had set, but the night was so transparent that the <u>white</u> house-fronts between the elms looked <u>gray</u> against the <u>snow</u>, clumps of bushes made <u>black</u> stains on it, and the basement windows of the church sent shafts of *yellow* light far across the endless undulations (Mattie was inside the church).

WARM EXAMPLE:

She seemed to *melt* against him in her terror, and he caught her in his arms, held her fast there, felt her lashes beat his cheek like netted butterflies.

However, my favorite quote, that I remembered to jot down while reading, is this: "Instead, it sprang up to a gale which now and then, from a tattered sky, flung <u>pale</u> sweeps of sunlight over a landscape chaotically tossed." Wharton definitely has a great talent in descriptions, and I was amazed by her endless creativity in describing a landscape which would appear monotone to the normal eye.

I liked the way the narrator and Wharton began the story. As Ethan looked in the church window at Mattie and the dance, the reader "looked in" the narrator's "window" at the story of the mysterious man (Ethan Frome). Whether this was intentional or not, I liked the effect it created.

From the moment Ethan mentioned coasting and the dangerous elm tree, I knew that a combination of the two would be the cause for Ethan's limp and the demise of Mattie; I was wrong about the latter, as most of the other readers were mistaken in their predictions as to the ending. I thought Wharton truly surprised everyone by having Ethan and Mattie attempt to die together by crashing the sled into the infamous elm tree.

Skipping back to a previous scene, I thought the cat was a great way to symbolize Zeena's presence when Ethan and Mattie were home alone. Along with the stifling blanket of snow, these symbolic images reminded me of *Native Son*, where Bigger Thomas' murderous identity appears to be betrayed by the white cat that was a witness to his gruesome disposal of May's body.

I enjoyed Wharton's descriptions most of all, and as a result I find it difficult to fathom how others (including my brother) did not enjoy this.

—Alan

KEEPING TRACK OF LETTERS

As students wrote literary letters to their classmates, I did not collect the letters or keep track of them as many other teachers tried to do. Others believed I should read all the letters and evaluate them, sometimes by giving check minuses and check pluses. Whenever I received a letter from a student, I would look through the previous pages and count the letters to me and to peers. At the end of my response, I would record the numbers by writing something like (2+1) or (1+5) in the margin. I told the students that the first number in the parentheses indicated the number of letters to me and the second number referred to letters to classmates. Though I sometimes looked over students' letters to others, I did so to get an idea of what students were reading rather than to check up on how good the letters were. If a student was writing skimpy letters or others were answering with very brief replies, I would address the issue with those students at that time. Sometimes I told them that certain letters or replies were unacceptable and not in the spirit we had established, and I asked them to add more or to redo the letter. When it came to the end of the marking period and we were counting up the number of letters, I simply asked the students to turn to the last page on which I had recorded the count and we would resume counting from there. I never kept track of any of this information in a grade book. It was up to the students to keep this evidence in their literature logs. If they lost their logs, they would get no credit. Since teachers had to fill out a progress report on every student at the middle of each marking period, I would have the record for the first five weeks. Students who lost their notebooks after that point would have to reconstruct their work from that point on. This freed me from much needless record keeping and put the burden of proof where it belonged—with the students.

8 | FIGURING OUT EVALUATION

The best way for anyone to improve performance is to understand the reasons for success or failure. Tim Gallwey, author of *The Inner Game of Golf* (1979), discovered that the best way to evaluate golfers with varying abilities is to not give judgmental feedback. Players seem to do their best when they shut off their own judgmental mechanisms, what Gallwey calls Inner Self 1, the intellectual judgment that typically finds fault with the way players hit shots. Instead, Gallwey suggests that players focus on other factors, such as the number on the ball as it sits on the tee, or the dimples in the ball, or the scuff marks on it. When the mind focuses on these things, Inner Self 2 takes over and is free to hit the shot, making any necessary adjustments along the way. As a coach, Gallwey helped players find things to notice while they were going about hitting shots. He refrained from making judgmental statements such as "Nice shot" or "Don't worry. You'll get the next one." He believes that, when the critical voice of Inner Self 1 is turned off so that Inner Self 2 can take over, the natural instincts of any player who wants to be out playing in the first place will allow that player to be successful.

Like Gallwey's players, I discovered that if I removed myself from being the constant critic, I could allow students to make more intelligent decisions about their own work. I found that they responded to this change and enjoyed doing what was asked of them, particularly when it was their own work. The idea of allowing students more responsibility in an English class appealed to me a long time ago, but I began to experiment with it only after beginning to use a workshop format. I recall Donald Graves suggesting involving students in the evaluation process. He said that if we want to know what students can and can't do, we should start by asking them. I came to discover that it's possible to give students the criteria for making decisions about the work they choose to do and what changes they need to make along the way to keep them on course. At the end of the school year, when parents or students want to thank me for what I've done, I reply that they are the ones who did all the work—I just tried to get out of the way and to allow them room to operate, to run around, and to play. Like a coach who allows his quarterback to call the plays, my classroom environment required me to turn over much of the choice to the students. In the end, it freed me to troubleshoot areas that needed attention. Not having to evaluate every student on every detail, I found that students could be taught to do their own self-assessments, stating what they had accomplished and what their evaluation should be.

STARTING THE YEAR WITH GOALS

Some people find it astounding when I say that in the last ten years of teaching eighth through twelfth grades, I never put a grade on a single piece of writing. I also never gave a test or quiz on anything, including assigned reading. For the most part, I never assigned readings that had to be done by the next day. Students, with lives as busy as adults, had the ability to plan when they were going to do their reading.

After the first few days of class, I asked students about evaluation. My philosophy of learning told me that they would do better by not having each piece of writing graded but, if I didn't evaluate everything they did each day, how could we handle the end of the marking period when the school wanted me to turn in grades? If I gave no tests to evaluate what they were reading, what should we do? What we always arrived at, through negotiation, was an evaluation process that took almost a week at the end of each marking period to complete.

We agreed that a reasonable goal for reading was one hundred pages a week from books they chose and from those we might read as a class. This number took into account that students would have time to read in class but were also expected to do reading at home. If they read ten pages in school and ten pages at home during the week, they would complete the hundred pages. In addition, we agreed that one literary letter a week was fair, totaling ten for a ten-week quarter. Each literary letter included two quoted excerpts from the text of the book they were reading and approximately five hundred words of their own thoughts about the book. Each letter would be followed by a response from the teacher or classmates. We agreed that completing two pages a week in the writer's notebook would not be a burden, for a total of twenty pages for the quarter. Sometimes we used the writer's notebooks in class for the minilesson and sometimes students wrote in them at home. We also agreed that a finished piece of writing every seven to eight days was reasonable, which amounted to six or seven finished pieces per quarter, polished and typed. We agreed that if a student met all these requirements to the very best of his or her ability, regardless of how the work compared to that of anyone else in the class, that student would get an A+, the highest possible grade.

One benefit was that students knew at the start of the quarter what the ground rules were, what they were expected to do. Some critics might argue that this evaluation process was still a "numbers game," and in a way I guess it was. And yet, students were free to make choices about when and how to accomplish their work—and what they wanted to accomplish. It was all predicated on treating students, as closely as possible, like real writers and real readers rather than as just students who had to do assigned reading and writing. The students didn't always manage their time well, but they learned about responsibility and what happens when time is mismanaged, just as we all do.

Joe Quattrini, a friend of mine from upstate New York, changed the way assessment took place in his classes as a result of a student's comment after an unscheduled fire drill. After the class had settled down to take a test, the fire bell rang and the class went outside for the drill. On the return trip, a girl said, "Mr. Quattrini, it isn't fair! I knew all of the material when I first came into the room but now I forget it." Joe said that it suddenly became clear to him that "anything that could be forgotten during the time of a fire drill was not worth testing in the first place."

QUARTERLY PORTFOLIOS

According to our agreement at the start of the year, students would spend time looking back at their writing near the end of each marking period, reflecting on their work and collecting it into a polished format—revised, edited, and typed. Evaluation would depend on their pointing out the skills and strategies that they'd learned. For example, we agreed that students should have six or seven finished pieces during each ten-week period. Of course, this wouldn't work out for all students. Some may have fewer long pieces. Some may have a collection of poems, an expository essay, and an eight-page short story. The actual collections varied with each student, what work we'd done as a whole class, and the kinds of writing I brought to their attention during the mini-lessons.

While students collected and polished, I handed out a portfolio evaluation cover sheet to be stapled to the other pieces of writing and handed in at the end of the marking period (see Figure 8–1). On this sheet, students list the title, the genre, and the number of words or lines (in a poem) for each piece of writing that's in the portfolio, ranking the pieces in their order of importance to them. Then they write a three- or four-sentence reflection about each piece, which gives them the opportunity to think about each piece after time has passed. They record the origin of the piece, the ease or difficulty of completion, their plans for the piece, its importance to them, and any particular skill or strategy that they used in writing it. When students select work for their final portfolios and need to write reflections, the quarterly reflections serve as a place to start.

The reverse side of the cover prompts students to think about their work in a different way (see Figure 8–2). One prompt says, "The Piece I Would Like to Burn." Of course, students don't actually burn papers, but the prompt acknowledges that some pieces might not work for one reason or another

English 11H Portfolio Evaluation

Mr. Mahoney   **1st Quarter:**   Date_____   Name_____

Fill these out carefully now to save work at the end of the year.   *Look for pictures now!*

A. Listed below are the titles of pieces I've written this quarter, ranked in order
   of their importance to me, followed by a reflection (history of piece) on each one:

#1. Most Important and Why ————————————————————————————
| Type of Writing – # of words |

#2. Most Important and Why ————————————————————————————
| Type of Writing – # of words |

#3. Most Important and Why————————————————————————————
| Type of Writing – # of words |

#4. Most Important and Why————————————————————————————
| Type of Writing – # of words |

#5. Most Important and Why————————————————————————————
| Type of Writing-# of words |

#6. Most Important and Why————————————————————————————
| Type of Writing |

FIGURE 8–1. *Quarterly Portfolio Evaluation (Side 1)*   **141**

Name ═══════════════════ ◯

B. Choose a paper for each of the following categories and explain your choice.

1. "Most Difficult to Write"   Paper # ___ Why?_ _ _ _ _ _ _ _ _ _ _ _ _ _ _ _ _ _
_ _

2. "Most Enjoyable to Write" Paper # ___ Why?_ _ _ _ _ _ _ _ _ _ _ _ _ _ _ _ _ _
_ _

3. "The Piece I Would Like to Burn" (or work on more, or turn into a poem,
get more help on)   Paper # ___   Why? _
_ _

C. My 5 – 6 pieces of writing in polished, final drafts, are numbered consecutively from
most important to least important, and they are stapled together. **On each paper,** I
have labeled in the margin and have highlighted some examples of what I've learned or
can do. From all the papers, there are twelve areas indicating my skill/ growth:

1. an effective title– creates an image
2. an effective "lead"
3. a major re-"vision" (adding signif. details)
4. Revising by cutting back (compression)
5. transitional sentence
6. my best example of "showing, not telling."
7. a modifier before or after the base sentence
8. an appositive (noun explaining noun)
9. strong verbs
10. my best sentence
11. Begin a sentence with a participial phrase
12. Evidence of a punctuation rule learned
13. Developing a character w/ strong traits
14. Establishing a clear, effective setting
15. Evidence of improving appearance of writing
    such as Pagemaker, shadows & reverse text

16. simile
17. metaphor
18. Alliteration
19. Taking a writing risk
20. other fig. language
21. other writing tools
22. a line or word that I
    got from someone else
23. epigraph, allusion, or ext. metaphor
24. Evidence of peer/teacher help
25. free verse, blank verse
26. rhythm or rhyme scheme
27. other things taught in lessons
    or known
28. Absolute (noun + part of verb)

> *I realize this is my time to show that I know some things and can do some things. Now is the time where I show this by identifying 10 areas and then explaining in the margin why each thing that I've identified is really that. The neat thing is that I get to show what I want to show.*

Showing Your Stuff

D. In the space remaining, explain one or two areas of growth or accomplishment that
you are most proud of.

So. . . . tell me what was great . . . .

142   FIGURE 8–2.   *Quarterly Portfolio Evaluation (Side 2)* and are frustrating. Even then, a time may come when writers return to a part of the paper, or all of it, to use it for spare parts.

On the bottom of the sheet is a list of skills and strategies for writing, ranging from effective leads to appositives, from parallel structure to symbols and metaphor. I ask students to select ten or twelve of these skills (or add some that aren't on the list), then identify where each can be found in their writing by going into their texts, marking them up, identifying the words or sentences, using a highlighter, and then annotating this marked text to explain why the work demonstrates the skills they say it does. For example, a student might contend that a piece's lead was effective because "it uses action to get the reader into the middle of an important event and to feel the power of the action." Or that something is an example of an extended metaphor because "it introduces the image of a baseball game of catch in each of the stanzas and yet is suggesting a dialogue or communication between the father and son on more than just baseball."

Applying Graves' suggestion about asking students to show what they know, I want students to be able to point out in their own work the skills that make a piece successful. I don't want this demonstration to be on a test about leads or metaphors or appositives. With tests, there is never any assurance that the skill is going to be transferred to the writing, put into practice. Asking students to show in their writing what they know engages them in metacognition, the act of thinking about their thinking. Using the quarterly portfolio is more time-efficient than administering and marking tests throughout the year. See Figures 8–3, 8–4, and 8–5 for examples of Sheila's quarterly portfolio cover sheet and an example of how she marked up her writing.

OTHER ASPECTS OF EVALUATION

At the beginning of evaluation week, I distribute an evaluation form (Figures 8–6 and 8–7). By the end of the first quarter, I ask students general questions about their perceptions of themselves as readers and how they can get better. The same three questions are then rephrased for writing. Students identify the traits of good readers and writers, judge themselves in terms of these qualities, then identify people (other students, the teacher) who can move them toward the ideals of the first question. While students are evaluating the previous quarter, they also develop general goals for the next quarter.

On the back of the evaluation sheet (Figure 8–7) are places for students to list the books and number of pages they read during the quarter and the pieces they wrote and their length. Students are asked to make judgments by ranking the books in order of importance to them. At this point, I tell my students the story of Betty Osk. She and her brother had a tradition of arranging the books they received for Christmas according to the order they planned to read them in. Betty would keep shifting the order around, anticipating with great delight devouring each book, moving a book from one spot

English 11H Portfolio Evaluation

⑥

Mr. Mahoney | 1st Quarter | **Date**_____   **Name** Sheila Erimez

Fill these out carefully now to save work at the end of the year.

Look for pictures now!

A. Listed below are the titles of pieces I've written this quarter, ranked in order of their importance to me, followed by a reflection (history of piece) on each one:

#1. Most Important and Why The Space

| Type of Writing – # of words |
| PROSE – 487 |

I think writing this piece was "good for me". It helped me to get out some of those "I miss you" blues, and "capture" some fond memories on paper. This was a very spontaneous piece, and I think it turned out to be one of the best things I've written so far. I'm very proud of this piece, & I even mailed it to Aaron

NOT 4 E.N.

#2. Most Important and Why Corroded

| Type of Writing – # of words |
| Poem – 365 |

This piece is important to me, because although I feel some parts could be improved, it really sums up my feelings on this horrible topic. It was a good "release" for me, and it was indeed very difficult to write. Though I'm not particularly happy about the actual content of the poem, I'm glad I was able to express the intensity in it.

NOT 4 E.N.

#3. Most Important and Why Drained

| Type of Writing – # of words |
| poem – 135 |

Another "release" poem. As you might have guessed, I went through some "tough times" in the past year, and this poem is important to me because it expresses the hurt and anger I felt. I wrote about some pretty touchy themes this quarter, and this is one of them. It was hard to write this, too.

#4. Most Important and Why Dance in the Rain

| Type of Writing – # of words |
| Prose – 310 |

Ahh... a happy memory. This actually started as an entry in my journal. I'm not really sure why I wrote this in the "third person" – maybe I wanted to turn it into a kind of "legend" or something. Maybe I just wanted to make it a story that others could "fill in with their own name". Who knows. It made for a nice "childhood memory" – a nice break from #2 and #3.

#5. Most Important and Why To My Dearest Aaron

| Type of Writing – # of words |
| Letter – 503 |

OK – you're probably thinking, "What the heck is a trivial little letter like this doing in here?" Well, I'll tell ya – variety is the very spice of life, and I think this is a great, lively little number. Sometimes being able to write freely like this is good for you – it opens you up to different styles, and gives you some practice at writing humorously. It's an important part of a balanced literary diet.

NOT FOR E.N.

#6. Most Important and Why One Summer Plea

| Type of Writing |
| poem – 359 |

Here we have another pleasant childhood memory. Yes – its an ok poem, but I just don't think it worked out. It was a decent attempt, and a few good things came out of it, but some things are meant to be "just memories in your head", and I think this is one of them.

144   FIGURE 8–3.   *Sheila Erimez' Quarterly Evaluation Portfolio (Side 1)*

Name <u>Sheila Erimez</u>

B. Choose a paper for each of the following categories and explain your choice.

1. "Most Difficult to Write" Paper # <u>2</u> Why? <u>I don't like writing about such</u> <u>touchy topics – I had to deal with a lot of nasty feelings.</u>

2. "Most Enjoyable to Write" Paper # <u>5</u> Why? <u>I felt no pressure writing</u> <u>letters to Aaron, & they show my lighter, humorous side, which</u> is fun to write with.

3. "The Piece I Would Like to Burn" (or work on more, or turn into a poem, get more help on) Paper # <u>6</u> Why? <u>This is that one piece you get</u> <u>every quarter that just kinda falls flat on its butt. It sounds</u> like something I'd write back in Jr. High! Ah! That can be scary.

C. My 5 – 6 pieces of writing in polished, final drafts, are numbered consecutively from most important to least important, and they are stapled together. **On each paper**, I have labeled in the margin and have highlighted some examples of what I've learned or can do. From all the papers, there are twelve areas indicating my skill/ growth:

1. an effective title– creates an image
2. an effective "lead"
3. a major re-"vision" (adding signif. details)
4. Revising by cutting back (compression)
5. transitional sentence
6. my best example of "showing, not telling."
7. a modifier before or after the base sentence
8. an appositive (noun explaining noun)
9. strong verbs
10. my best sentence
11. Begin a sentence with a participial phrase
12. Evidence of a punctuation rule learned
13. Developing a character w/ strong traits
14. Establishing a clear, effective setting
15. Evidence of improving appearance of writing such as Pagemaker, shadows & reverse text

16. simile
17. metaphor
18. Alliteration
19. Taking a writing risk
20. other fig. language
21. other writing tools
22. a line or word that I got from someone else
23. epigraph, allusion, or ext. metaphor
24. Evidence of peer/teacher help
25. free verse, blank verse
26. rhythm or rhyme scheme
27. other things taught in lessons or known
28. Absolute (noun + part of verb)

I realize this is my time to show that I know some things and can do some things. Now is the time where I show this by identifying 10 areas and then explaining in the margin why each thing that I've identified is really that. The neat thing is that I get to show what I want to show.

Showing Your Stuff

D. In the space remaining, explain one or two areas of growth or accomplishment that you are most proud of.

So, . . . tell me what was great . . . .

I am glad that I was able to write about some pretty "hard-core" stuff this quarter. I wasn't too comfortable writing about certain "nasty" subjects, but I think they came out well, even though they deal with "unpleasant" things. I'm also glad I could write something fit to be sent to my brother (The Space) Nothin' like showing your sibling you miss him. My pieces of writing varied greatly this quarter – I think I showed a lot of different styles and moods, and that's a good thing. One should be able to write in different ways, and be "flexible" with writing.

FIGURE 8–4. *Sheila Erimez' Quarterly Evaluation Portfolio (Side 2)*

The Space

I notice it sometimes at the dinner table, which now seats three, not four. I notice it in the long silences between petty news, when all I hear is the scrape of knives on plates and gulps of drink. I notice it sometimes on quiet early mornings, when Mom has overslept, and I am the only one up and about, making all the noise there is to be made...which is not much. Aaron used to make the morning noises that would announce the start of a new day — his 6AM shower. It always woke me up, and gave me a reason to get out of bed — someone else was up and at 'em, groggy as me, but still ready to face the dawn. It was kind of comforting, knowing that someone else was struggling into the morning with me — my brother, too, had to push back the blanket and find, in some inch of his body, the strength and the will to rise from a warm, snug bed.

It was nicer with him at the dinner table, too. We three have sort of lost our "symmetry" without him. He and Dad would talk and talk and talk...sometimes getting on each other's nerves, but always in a bond. And even if I couldn't get a word in, I never realized how good it was just to listen to their voices. Sometimes Aaron and I would exchange an "inside joke" that was too quick for Dad to catch — we liked to keep him in the dark every now and then, just for the fun of it, and because it was a "brother-sister" thing.

I remember times last year in the school hallway when I'd happen to come across his path. Sometimes, if he didn't see me, I'd poke him in the ribs or tussle his hair. If we both saw each other, though, we'd either bump the other "accidentally" or have an affectionate exchange of "name-calling." We'd always pass with a smile.

I notice it, sometimes, in the hallways now...should I see the face of a freshman who carries in his eyes the same spirit of his older, past-graduated brother. I think of Aaron, in his perfect blue cap and gown, with the all-American tassel swinging off the side.

I notice it — I notice the space in my house...in the hall...in my life. I notice the quiet where there used to be sound...not often...mostly I'm too busy to hear it...but once in a while, when things slow to a mosey...I hear his absence...and I see it in what is not there. Sometimes I fear I don't know him...I fear he's gone out like a flame and turned into something I won't recognize. Then I hear his broken laugh, or I see the split in his lower lip...and I can call him "nitz," and walk past on my way down the hall, smiling.

(1)

Evaluation Conference Notes

FIRST QUARTER

English __11h__

Estimated grade

A /

NAME *Sheila Erimez* 8 wonderful letters - full of *zest* not one # - one miss ⑥
literary letters not answered
(2 + 6)
prose pieces (4)
Poems (3)
looseleaf binder/cl. notes (17)
books read (5)
pages read (1133)
Writer's NB pages (20) *gw*

WRITING

1. What does it take to be a good writer?

A good writer is willing to take risks in his/her writing. A good writer tries to improve his/her skills in every piece of writing, and enjoys the creations they make.

2. How good a writer are you?

I like to think that I'm a pretty good writer. I put a lot of time and care into each piece I write. Sometimes I'm very pleased with the result, & sometimes I'm disgusted. But either way, I take what I've learned & keep at it.

3. What have you learned to make you a better writer?

I've learned that you can't be afraid to write about "touchy" subjects, or things that you're afraid to expose - often the best writing comes from topics you feel strongly about. Also, if you get a sudden inspiration - I don't care where you are - find a pen & paper & get it out in ink before it's gone.

4. GOALS
What do you want to learn or do to be or show yourself as a better writer? Who in this class can help you?

I'd like to be able to write my poems more metaphorically - sometimes they can sound a bit too much like prose. Laura is excellent at metaphors - I could learn from her writing (Her "clock" metaphor poem was incredible in 9th grade)

5. What risks did you take as a writer? Explain.

As a writer, I finally took risks in writing about subjects that I wasn't so sure I wanted on paper. They turned out to be some of my best pieces.

READING

1. What does it take to be a good reader?

A good reader likes to read a variety of book types, and can enjoy each one for what it is. A good reader also reads with "zest" - he/she soaks up and thoroughly enjoys what they read

2. How good a reader are you?

I think I'm a pretty average reader. I'm somewhat picky when it comes to choosing a book to read, but if it's the right one for me - I'll read it nonstop.

3. What have you learned to make you a better reader?

I've learned that, yes - classics are good for you. There's a reason why they call them "classics". I noticed that reading such books has a positive effect on my writing, so I try to absorb what I read so I can "implement" it in

4. GOALS my writing.
What do you want to learn or do to be or show yourself as a better reader? Who in this class can help you?

I'd like to actually make the time to read! (I'm a very busy woman!) Also, I think it's important that I take more risks and read books that I don't usually read. Rob Wahl is an extraordinary reader - perhaps he could give me some suggestions.

5. What risks did you take as a reader? Explain.

As I reader, I took a risk with Pilgrim - it was a very unusal kind of book, but I read it from cover to cover anyway, and I learned a lot from it.

On the back. list the titles of your writing and reading.

FIGURE 8–6. *Sheila Erimez' Evaluation Conference Notes—First Quarter (Side 1)*

Writing

List below the writing you did this marking period in order of importance to you, from most important to least important.

Title	type / length
(7) 1. Seamus Heaney's "Digging": Walking the Same Footsteps on Another Path.	Literary analysis / 1,151 words
2.	
(3) Drained	poem / 135 words
(1) The Space	prose / 487 words
(2) Corroded	poem / 365 words
5.	
(4) Dance in the Rain	prose / 310 words
(5) To My Dearest Aaron	letter / 503 words
8. One Summer Plea (6)	poem / 359 words
9.	
10.	
11.	
12.	

Reading

List below the things you've read that you are happiest at having read, from greatest joy to least.

Title	Author	type / length
(3) 1. To Kill A Mockingbird	Harper Lee	classic / novel / 281
2. Ethan Frome (1)	Edith Wharton	classic / novel / 133
(2) 3. Pilgrim At Tinker Creek	Annie Dillard	personal observations of natural world / 271
4. Edith Wharton (5)	Margaret B. McDowell	literary criticism / 30
5. The Hot Zone (4)	Richard Preston	non-fiction / 418
6.		
7.		
8.		
9.		
10.		
11.		
12.		

FIGURE 8–7. *Sheila Erimez' Evaluation Conference Notes—First Quarter (Side 2)*

to the next, reconfiguring the great plan. I suggest that ranking—thinking
back about the many books they have read in the quarter and putting them
in order of importance to them—can be fun.

I remember Anne, who put *The Joy Luck Club* first in her list because she
and her mother had read it at the same time and were able to converse about
it. She wrote that the bond between her mother and her was important to her,
and the book symbolized that communication. Another student, Alan, placed
Nineteen Eighty-Four first because his older brother, Eric, had loved the book
years ago. Now that Alan had finally read it, he loved it for the connection
with his brother it gave him. Dave read *Chinese Handcuffs* because his girlfriend was reading it and had asked him to read it with her. Keri once thought
the classics boring, but as she was developing a power for reading widely,
she decided to read nothing but classics one quarter. Amazed that they were
not necessarily boring, she had difficulty putting one book above another
but eventually settled on *Jane Eyre* as the book that she loved the most. Erick
listed S. E. Hinton's *The Outsiders* as his most important book because he
saw how Johnny Cade's beatings by his father were just like Erick's but that
the humiliation of words was far more scarring than any beatings. He saw
for the first time someone else, in the form of a character in a story, saying
something that he himself had felt for years. Having students rank and rate
books, rethink the books in light of other books, and place them in a hier-
archy affords an opportunity for reflection at the end of the marking period
that is important for growth and insight.

RANKING WRITING

Just as students list books read, number of pages, and the author on the evaluation sheet, they do the same on the other half of the page for the pieces of
writing done during the marking period. Mary ranked her literary analysis as
most important to her because she worked the hardest on that piece. Mike
agreed because it was such an intimidating task at first. Ray, too, chose the literary analysis, because he had never understood how to "dig out the hidden
meaning that teachers often seem to dream up," as he put it; by doing the
analysis, he had learned a system for opening up texts by himself. These three
students gained a feeling of power and accomplishment by writing the literary analysis. Other students might list a personal story or a poem first because
it allowed them to unburden themselves of feelings that were troubling them.
Still others might list pieces written as gifts, which they gave to someone on a
special occasion such as Valentine's Day, Mother's or Father's Day, or a birthday. The students all developed their own criteria for rating a paper as higher
or lower, and this critical ability grew out of being given the opportunity and
the requirement to reflect on their writing during the marking period. All of
the students completed the set number of pieces, but their rankings were individual and reflected little of what a teacher might have thought best.

After evaluating the work done in the first marking period, I ask my students if they are satisfied with what they've accomplished. I ask them what they need to know to be more successful in the second marking period. I distribute a half-sheet of paper and ask them to write down what they want me to teach or reteach so that they can be successful.

Some teachers give tests to find out how much students have retained, but it seems much more respectful and direct to ask them what they believe they need to learn or relearn. Invariably, I'm shocked by the things that students tell me they don't understand and want more help on. Some are things that I may have completely forgotten to do and some are things that they just want more elaboration on. When you repeat the writing/reading workshop for several years, some of the lessons become part of a routine and fit in certain places in the year. For this reason, I try to be vigilant about not letting my lessons become institutionalized because "it has always been done that way." That's why I find it particularly helpful to return to my students for reminders of what they need. Once they give me this feedback and I decide what needs to be done the next day, I return to class and thank them for their help and apologize for any omissions. They always seem to sense my appreciation for their honesty and they begin to feel empowered because they have a stake in how their class runs and how their learning will progress. The next step is even more important. I do a minilesson on whatever most students have indicated they need help with. After that, I announce that I would like to meet in a corner of the room with a specific group of students about another topic. Then I say that I'll be teaching a specific skill, such as using quotes with dialogue, during the last part of the period and that anyone who wants to can join in for that lesson. This shows the students that I am ready to act promptly on their expressed needs. Indirectly, I am saying that we need to keep communicating about what is going well and what is not.

The work I do with reviewing and elaborating skills for student success in the workshop sets the stage for students to set goals for themselves for the next quarter. I ask them to list what they would like to learn or accomplish in the next ten weeks. In addition, I pass out a worksheet that summarizes the four New York State learning standards (Figure 8–8). New York's standards are similar to most states' and to the national standards developed by the NCTE and the IRA. In general, they state that students should be able to read, write, speak, and listen for a variety of purposes. The worksheet includes a brief description of the four learning standards in English/language arts:

1. Using Language for Information and Understanding
2. Using Language for Literary Response and Expression
3. Using Language for Critical Analysis and Evaluation
4. Using Language for Social Action

English Language Arts

Name _____

Quarter 3

Grade Level __8__

Reading	Writing
Speaking	Listening

Goal Setting

using the 4
NYS Learning Standards

Standard 1:
Using Language for INFORMATION & UNDERSTANDING: (collecting data, facts, ideas through research: interviews, surveys, panels, research papers/reports/debates)

1. Read my manual and talk with my father so that I can get my modem working and can send email to Mr. Mahoney.

2. Read and study collections of poems by a female author so that I can make my own collection of about five to six poems on a topic.

3. Conduct a survey or interview 6–7 of my friends and 3–4 teachers to see what issues they think are most important to write about for kids my age.

4. Read a "How To" book on the Mac and then ask Mr. Mahoney so I can use my Mac better and figure out what I can do with it.

Standard 2:
Using Language for LITERARY RESPONSE & EXPRESSION: (responding to literature [lit. letters], literary essays, writing metaphorically, writing creatively: poems, short stories, plays, story telling, etc.)

1. Create my own collection of poems that express a theme like friendship and give this to my three good friends.

2. Write a 1000-word short story on a single incident of a character in conflict or having to make a decision.

3. Read 4–5 short stories by contemporary writers to see how they handle characters in conflict.

4. Read aloud work done in writing minilesson to gain confidence in my reading.

Standard 3:
Using Language for CRITICAL ANALYSES & EVALUATION: (literary analysis, critical reviews, editorials, position papers, scientific inquiries, reviewing and revising papers and presentations)

1. Read the works of my two favorite authors (Lois Duncan and M. H. Clark), read about their lives in references books in the library, and write a report of analysis of how their styles are the same or different.

2. Improve my ability to write good, clear essays by writing a comparison/contrast paper on two sports stars. (Read for this information in 1st Standard.)

3. Learn 15 skills on the portfolio evaluation sheet so I can mark up my writing at least two weeks before the quarter ends. Discuss with Mr. Mahoney and ask questions in class each day.

Standard 4:
Using Language for SOCIAL ACTION: (invitations, personal and business letters, running meetings, creating invitations, email)

1. Try and fix up my computer so I can send email to Mr. Mahoney.

2. Write a letter to Lois Duncan, telling her what I like about her books and asking her a few questions.

3. Improve my listening skills with my friends so I can show real interest through my body language and face reactions.

4. Reduce the size of my handwriting so others can read my writing without struggling. Try to get 7–9 words on a line.

FIGURE 8–8. *Goal Setting*

We discuss whether students are addressing these standards in any of their other classes, and often discover that they are. Students then take the list of things that they want to accomplish and write them in the space provided on the worksheet for the particular standards, making realistic lists not only of what they want to do, but also of what they can get done in the given amount of time. I then ask them to indicate what evidence will tell whether they met their goals. Vague statements such as "become a better writer" are not really goals but wishes. We talk about goals being measurable in some way. For example, if a student conducts an interview of several people, he or she will write notes and then perhaps write about their findings. We can look at those notes or those pieces to see if the goals were met. Although I ask students to list on the worksheet an item in each standard as a starting point, they sometimes don't accomplish things in each standard during every marking period. They need to have worked in all four of the standards by the end of the year and they should not dwell on only one standard exclusively.

The first time I used this worksheet, I found that students were confused and misplaced their goals with the wrong standards. I took the goals that they had listed and placed each one with the correct standard. I prepared as a handout some of the corrected goals and showed this to all of my classes. I then asked students to revise their misplaced goals and standards, based on what they had learned in that lesson. Figure 8–8 shows my correct placement of the activities that my regular-track eighth graders had originally handed in as goals.

These students planned for the coming quarter by choosing goals and identifying activities to work on in the weeks ahead. They still had the general expectations of literary letters, pages read, and finished pieces from the first quarter, but in quarters two, three, and four, they had goals that they put into the learning standards. It is interesting to note how often the standards overlap each other. For example, under Standard 1 we see that the first goal of a student was to read and speak with his father to get information to solve his problem, but that outcome jumped to Standard 4—sending and receiving email from me. Student 2 was reading poetry (Standard 2), but the purpose wasn't for literary appreciation as much as it was to learn how to do the same thing herself (Standard 1) . . . but then it carried over into Standard 4 (social action) because she was going to give the poems to her three good friends. So, the same activity can fulfill multiple standards.

EVALUATION WITH GOAL SETTING

The evaluation sheets for the next three marking periods looked different because of the goal setting that students did for each quarter (see Figures 8–9 and 8–10). I resisted grading students on their goals because some would eventually learn that setting easier goals was one way to beat the system. As a result, I created an evaluation sheet that asked students to record anything

Evaluation Conference Notes
THIRD QUARTER
English 11 H

A   A+

Estimated Grade

| A+ | the Best! |

NAME Sheila Erimez   # ⑥

		B	B+	A	A+
literary letters- Tr			1	2	②
Peers		5	6	7	③
Prose pieces		3	4	5	6
Poems		3	4	5	6
Books read		2	3	4	5
pages read		800	1000	1200	1200+
Writer's NB pages		10	15	20	20✗
Class Participation					
Attendance		5-6	2-4	1-2	0-2

List titles below:

Literary Analysis-*Gatsby*: Gatsby's Green Light: The Foolish American Dream

Walt Whitman Poem: Sounds of Exploration

Expository Essay: The Wish

Non-fiction book: Hiroshima

Lit. Letter Home: Dear Mommy

Gatsby Passages: pgs 189, 171

What accomplished in the 4 Standards? List below what you can show to support your work in each standard.

| WRITING | READING | SPEAKING | LISTENING |

Standard 1:
Using Language for INFORMATION & UNDERSTANDING:
(collecting data, facts, ideas through research: interviews, surveys, panels, research papers/reports/debates)

1.

2.

Standard 3:
Using Language for CRITICAL EVALUATION & ANALYSIS:
(literary analysis, critical reviews, editorials, positions papers, inquiries. Reviewing and revising papers and presentations)

1. I entered the realm of Standard 3 with my lit. analysis of Gatsby, which I'm quite proud of.

2.

Standard 2:
Using Language for LITERARY RESPONSE & EXPRESSION:
(responding to literature [lit. letters], literary essays, writing metaphorically, writing creatively: poems, short stories, plays, etc.; story telling)

1. As always, I've got tons of creative writing - The Wish is something I might give to Dad as a wee gift.

2.

Standard 4:
Using Language for SOCIAL INTERACTION: (interviews, personal & business letters, running meetings, e-mail)

1.

2.

What accomplishments are you most proud of? Explain.

I'm quite proud of my lit. analysis of Gatsby — though it may be somewhat short, it's "to the point" and pretty well-written. I also thought that The Wish came out decently, considering the amount of time I had to write it.

On the back, list the titles of your writing and reading.

What did you fail to accomplish and why?

Darn it, I still haven't read any poetry books- that's the 1st thing I'll do next quarter. There's simply not enough time to do a research paper. As far as the poetry goes, it seems there's always "something else I have to read first."

FIGURE 8–9. *Sheila Erimez' Evaluation Conference Notes—Third Quarter (Side 1)*   153

Writing

List below the writing you did this marking period in order of importance to you, from most important to least important.

Title	Type	Length
1. Solitaire	prose	185 words
2. The Wish	expository essay	372
3. Sounds of Exploration	poem	283
~~oops~~		
4. Gatsby's Green Light: The Foolish American Dream	literary analysis	total 500 (352)
5. Scenes from A Pier By The Pub	poem	125
6. Night Lights	poem	82

Reading

List below the things you've read this marking period in order of importance to you, from most important to least important.

Title	Type	Length	Author
1. A Farewell To Arms	Novel	314	Hemingway
2. Of Mice & Men	Novel	118	Steinbeck
3. Fahrenheit 451	Novel	179	Ray Bradbury
4. The Pearl	Novel	118	Steinbeck
5. The Great Gatsby	Novel	214	F.S. Fitzgerald
6. To Have & Have Not	Novel	262	Hemingway
7. Ernest Hemingway	Literary Criticism	30	Earl Rovit
8. Hiroshima	Non Fiction	116	John Hersey

154   FIGURE 8–10. *Sheila Erimez' Evaluation Conference Notes—Third Quarter (Side 2)* that they completed that could be included in one of the four standards and indicate any goals they didn't achieve and why. Finally, they were asked to indicate which, if any, of the goals they wanted to carry over to the next marking period.

WHAT ABOUT GRADES AND TESTS?

As I mentioned earlier, in the last ten years of my teaching, I have neither given a test nor put a grade on any single paper. I have asked my students if those who work get graded every day at jobs behind counters in fast-food chains, in supermarkets, in banks, or in hospitals. They all agree that no boss grades them every day or even very often. They never receive a letter or a number grade at work and rarely get a performance rating. Even teachers don't get rated with numbers or letters, but a written report of their strengths and weakness usually follows an observation. Some veteran teachers may go for years without a formal evaluation.

To those who believe in grades, I argue that if you don't work any harder or more easily because there's no grade given for your performance, and if you receive a paycheck at the end of the pay period even though there are no grades for you, what makes you think that students must be graded on everything they do in your class?

"Because we have to give a grade" is always the response. But just because we must give final grades in a marking period, it does not follow that we have to grade each and every move that students make. And yet some teachers want to have lots of grades for their students, so that they can justify the marking-period grades by pointing to the average of all this work. They think that they are being objective by having a list of numbers to be averaged. One would argue that the choice of what to test, what weight to put on some questions over others, and choosing some tests over others is a judgment call. Do spelling tests count as much as vocabulary tests? Do personal experience narratives carry as much weight as literary essays? How much should homework marks, quizzes, unit tests, and projects count in the final evaluation? Should we spend our time testing and marking so we can justify a grade?

Because I was young and popular, hardworking and organized, I was never challenged or asked to examine any of the pedagogical approaches I was taking. My administrators seemed to approach things pragmatically. Since I got good results, they left me alone. As I look back, I see that I was hiding behind testing, and I wonder how much real teaching was going on in my classroom. Through student teaching and my first six or seven years of teaching, I learned to survive and fortify myself with evaluations. And nobody complained.

So, then, is it a problem if I say that I don't need to give out grades as the marking period goes along, but instead wish to include students in the evaluation process by giving them guidelines and asking them to help say

how their learning has progressed? We've grown up in a society that evaluates students often, and assessment has reached a national craziness with state assessments in many subjects. Students in the assessment target grades, usually fourth, eighth, and eleventh, are subject to batteries of tests. If students are being tested so much, when do they get a chance to learn?

PORTFOLIO OR FINAL EXAM?

The first year that I presented the idea of using the portfolio as the final assessment to my ninth-grade class and my seventh-grade class, the students were ecstatic. "You mean we don't have to take a final exam when everyone else is taking one? Oh, man, that's great!" some of them said. Others said that their friends who had to take final tests would be jealous. "How will you grade us?" they asked. I told them that I wasn't exactly sure, but that it would be based on their showing me what they learned during the year in reading and writing or knew how to do. This might include skills that students had learned in a prior year but had only just mastered. In any case, I told them that we would work it all out and I would listen to them about what ways they could show me what they knew. Eventually, we decided that selecting five pieces of writing from all of the things that they had written during the year was a fair requirement. I said that there would be a series of additional reflections/explanations of this learning that would accompany these five pieces, as well as a sample of their best literary letter and some other things. As they worked away for weeks, most of the students were thrilled that they wouldn't have the dreaded final exam. They felt that they had gotten off easily with just a portfolio. Little did they know!

In addition to making portfolio covers, students spent the last weeks of the school year selecting and then revising the work that they thought represented their skill level and progress. Students generally seemed to be working diligently. Some saw that they either needed to or wanted to do some of this work at home, so they began to put in even more time on their "replacement final exam." Even as the due date approached, students were reporting spending great amounts of time at home on their portfolios. They weren't exactly complaining. Some were even boasting: "I was up to 12:30 last night doing my portfolio." Others indicated that they were getting into the project and actually enjoying it.

The following year the parent of an eighth grader called me and excitedly told me how much her son, a slow reader in the past, had gotten both her husband and her involved in typing the portfolio work for him. She wasn't complaining—she was seeing all the wonderful things her son had written and was marveling at all the books he had read. She was just wondering if the portfolio had to be perfect and if it had to be completely typed. I told her that it really should be the student's work, but if she wanted to help him type it (without correcting his errors) that was fine, but that it wasn't necessary for all the work to be typed. She said that her son insisted that it all be typed because he wanted it to be perfect. We had a good laugh at how this boy had been transformed as a reader and a writer and was cajoling his parents into involvement in the project.

Students continued in the final days to come to class and report the time spent the previous night. Many would add, "and my portfolio is going to be so good." On the last day of class, when students brought their finished portfolios in, I heard many ninth graders (and tenth graders the next year) talk about not having gone to bed so that they could put the final touches on their portfolios. I remembered how in previous years, I would be disappointed by some students' results on the final exam because they had failed to put in the necessary few hours needed to study. With the portfolios, students spent huge amounts of time completing their project/final exam and never complained; some actually found it fun.

FINAL CELEBRATIONS

There is nothing like a party to put a cap on things. Teams have victory parties, teachers have end-of-the-year parties, and many people have birthday parties. We do this to celebrate accomplishments and milestones. When students finish their portfolios, they have reason to be proud and I've used a variety of ways to celebrate that completion. The simplest way is to have students pass around their portfolios on the final day of class or on the day the portfolios are handed in, the way yearbooks are handled in some schools, providing opportunities for students to read and view the work of their classmates. Some students may even want to write a response in the back of a friend's portfolio. Another way of recognizing effort is to have students come to the front of the room and show their portfolio cover and explain the significance of the title. On the day that other students were taking the English final exam, my eight-grade class met and, for an hour and a half, students read each other's portfolios, gave short talks on their covers and themes, and read samples of the work in their collections. For that ninety-minute period, students listened, applauded, laughed, cried, and recognized each other as authors. No one seemed to notice when the buses began to assemble at the end of the day—the students had gained a sense of what authorship can be.

MY EVALUATIONS/RESPONSES

If my time to evaluate the portfolios was short, I would read through the collections and fill out a rating sheet before I had to return the portfolios a day or two later. At the bottom of the page, there was space for me to write three or four sentences of response. Often, though, the portfolios were so good and

I quickly saw that the student would receive the highest possible score of A+. I did not need to rush through the pages. I could linger over them, enjoying the wonderful work that students had done. I usually managed to hold back forty-five or fifty portfolios to spend more time with over the summer. Each day of the summer, I would read one or two of these works and then write a response. For my eleventh-grade students, who often asked me to write a letter of recommendation for them for college, I would use their portfolios as a basis for my comments and I would include the response sheet as part of the recommendation. One summer I wrote an individual poem as well as a prose commentary in response to each of the fifty portfolios. During another summer, for each student, I typed an appropriate poem or two from a published poet to accompany my prose response to their works. I placed these responses at the back of the portfolio but also gave the students multiple copies to include in their college application packets. By taking my time, I could be reminded of all the students had accomplished during the year, and I could savor their writing as well as the care and artistic skills they had used in putting together this work. Evaluation was the easy part for me. As Alan Lemley wrote in his portfolio, his grade had become a secondary consideration. Pride and satisfaction in the work had far more importance.

9 | MAKING SENSE OF HIGH-STAKES TESTING

My mother was an elementary school teacher—teaching seems to be in the family genes—but she died when my son Brian was almost seven. In fact, all four of his grandparents died before Brian reached age eight. Brian longs to speak to the people who would tell stories of the past the way his father and mother never did. And he needs to have his ancestors speak to him, so he has developed an obsession with tracing his ancestry back to Timothy Edward Mahoney, the one who "jumped the pond" to arrive in America in the 1850s. If Brian can connect with this illusive figure, his search for his own roots will lead him to Ireland.

It was never unusual for Brian to be thinking of the past. However, on one particular Veterans Day, home from his third year of teaching in a Florida fifth-grade classroom, he was experiencing frustration with all the impositions and obstacles to teaching and learning. That morning in 1995 he sat down to vent his frustrations in a poem. The images he created are ones that most teachers know intimately: the administrators who "change their charge" depending on the change in wind direction; the politicians who act like eggheads but who have no practical experience; the kids who are raised on pizza, the Simpsons, and "other electronic devices," as Bill Moyers says. Brian wondered if there had ever been a time when the battles were of a different sort, the kind that didn't leave teachers with nightmares and a feeling of never being able to do enough. At the heart of current teacher tribulation is the ever-present bludgeon of high-stakes testing.

Between Veterans

Dear Grandma,
The archives say you did
your tours at St. Gregory, the Great
in the 50's on and on.
I seized that at first, when I felt
called; when I joined up, and then
on Dad, who served the Commack
district and commanded.

"And I'll teach too," my instincts said.
I have seen some action now. I
find me purple-hearted, wrung riddled,
only three years in the trenches.
My troops won't fight; it's not a video,
or they look for me to 'get it' for them.
My generals change the charge
for each egg-head election,
leaving strategy to Personnel.
My country calls me baby-killer,
Chanting, "TEACH THE TEST,"
waving burning 'Progress' cards,
digesting pizza and the Simpsons
at the family hour. They want to win,
but can not make the conference.
Thank goodness we 'get summers off'
To detach and oil our prosthetic psyches.
I have seen some horror, here.
I wonder how your front held up, and
if you bled less fracturing or more.
I wonder if our nightmares are the same.

There are many fine books on the subject of the tyranny of testing. Certainly Susan Ohanian's *One Size Fits Few* (1999) and Alfie Kohn's *The Case Against Standardized Testing* (2000) present the issues and fallacies very well. Teachers need to be very aware of the insidious effects tests have had on students in grades all across the country. More than that, they need to devote some time and energy to educate parents about the impact and to get them involved in bringing pressure on their elected officials. Teachers are caught in a bind because they are faced with pressures from their superiors, who in turn are faced with directives and edicts. While teachers are working to change the system, they can also help their students get through the testing craze with as little anxiety as possible.

HOW MUCH TIME?

One teacher told me that her district had the eleventh-grade teachers do so much preparation for "the big test" in January that the students had begun to hate their teachers and their subject; the teachers felt the same toward the students and the material. The teacher realized that it was horrible but that they had no choice if they wanted to raise the scores.

I, too, faced this issue with the state test and even with the AP exam that my eleventh graders took. I never emphasized the test. I simply explained that at some point in the year, students would be taking the test and that we would stop what we were doing and look at old tests to figure out how to be successful on them. I never wanted the value of reading and writing to be seen as culminating in a test. I wanted students to see that the powerful experiences they were having all year had their own intrinsic worth and still allowed them to do very well on the tests. That is always what the results proved. I charted the scores on these tests from a time before we began using the workshop right on through my final year of teaching, and I discovered a significant increase on test scores. This improvement involved students in honors classes as well as struggling students in remedial classes.

Three weeks before the test administration date, we would look at examples of previous tests, trying to figure out what would be hard and what would be easy. One student, looking at the AP test for the first time in mid-April, exclaimed, "We've been doing this all year with the literary letters and our treatment of style! This should be easy!" In fact, she got a 4 on the test. Would her score have been any higher if I had started preparing for this test in September? I strongly believe that it wouldn't have, but even if it could have, my students and I agreed that we wouldn't trade the drudgery of test preparation for the rich literary experiences we had had all year.

So we figured out what the difficulties of the test were and set up a plan for mastering them. We decided which sections we should cover and in which order to treat them. I passed out models that had been scored in the past so we could look at what made a strong paper good and why a weak paper failed. We examined the rubrics that were provided and translated the criteria into student language. Then I asked the students to put away all of their materials and start to do the task on their own, beginning with the planning. I asked them to compare their notes, and I showed various ways of developing plans, including my own. Students selected plans closest to their own and used the information to continue developing their own writing. I was guiding them in the task, rather than assigning a task and marking it. I wanted each step of the process to be clear as students moved through the stages. I provided guided practice all along the way.

Then I asked students to write their introductory paragraph. We examined several different student examples and compared them to our "anchor" or model papers, noting the strengths of the high anchors and the deficiencies of the low ones. At that point, students went back and revised what they had written, based on what they had learned. Scaffolding like this is a way of advancing students step-by-step in a skill in the way any coach introduces a new drill or a parent teaches a child to tie a shoe or brush her teeth.

When students finished the task, I didn't take the pile of papers home to evaluate or grade. Instead, I moved students into groups of four, asking them to read each other's finished papers and apply the scoring rubric, adding a brief commentary about the papers. The students were very accurate in applying the criteria and assessing the papers. Then we came back as a class to discuss the difficulties and reflect on their new approaches and options. For each of the writing tasks, we would take a couple days to walk through the parts of the test. As a final tune-up, I asked students which task they wanted to work on and had them answer one task completely. Then I collected the papers and read them quickly, giving them a holistic score. The next day in class, students who needed a conference and those who wanted a meeting with me would get together, sometimes individually and sometimes in small groups. The work that students did in preparation for these tests never influenced their grade for the quarter. That was always based on the evaluation process outlined in the previous chapter. The test preparation was designed to allow students to do as well as they could and then return to their important learning. One of the by-products of this preparation was an understanding of how to figure out what a test was asking and how to answer successfully. Learning how to take a test is a valuable skill. That is quite different from drilling endlessly for a test.

In New York Stare, eighth graders take a test similar to the Regents exam eleventh-grade English students take. Some middle schools have become so nervous about how they will fare on the public report card printed in the newspapers that they begin testing and drilling students in sixth and seventh grade. Often they do the opposite of the process I suggested. They make up simulated tests and administer them on a schoolwide basis. Then the teachers score the tests, leaving students with a substitute teacher for a day or two. When all is said and done, the school receives scores that most teachers could have predicted, based on their own observations of classroom performance. Schools use the results to pull weaker students out of other classes for AIS (academic intervention services) or more drills. Some schools don't stop at that. Because a school's "report card" standing is affected by the higher scores as well, stronger students, having jumped the bar, aren't exempt from scrutiny. They must jump it by a sizeable amount in order to bring up the school's score. As a result, even the brighter students are put through drills to increase their scores, taking time away from other far more valuable work. This is one of the very issues that echoes in the subtitle of Alfie Kohn's book: *The Case Against Standardized Testing: Raising the Scores, Ruining the Schools.* Even the better students are victimized by the school's need to look good (or not to look too bad) on the report card. It's like a company reporting on its corporate profit for the year: The stockholders don't want to know about anything but the bottom line. Whether the company is making a product that is good for society is not important; only the numbers mean anything.

Fortunately, most parents disagree with this kind of testing. They trust the scores and reports generated by their children's schools and teachers, rather than by these one-shot tests. It is up to teachers, then, to give good feedback to parents. I felt very comfortable showing parents the evaluation sheets that I used. It was much more meaningful to parents than hearing a teacher read a list of thirty-five scores from a grade book. Both give evidence that is irrefutable when a student is performing up to my standards. The problem is that thirty-five scores in a grade book do not suggest any way to help, other than for the student to "straighten up."

My suggestion for easing the pressures of this testing frenzy is to help students and their parents make sense of the tests and to show what the scores mean and don't mean. Help them figure it out.

10 | FOOD FOR THE MIND AND SOUL

During a recent visit to the dentist, I noticed different techniques and improved equipment that were not present seven years ago when I had my last root canal. Last year I underwent a colonoscopy to detect any precancerous growths; ten years ago, such a procedure was not widely used and not nearly as perfected as it has become. These improvements wouldn't have been available to me if my doctors and dentists had not furthered their knowledge by attending seminars and conferences. The same is true of my auto mechanic, Jim Bruno, who goes to seminars to keep up with advances in today's engines. If he had the attitude "I know enough about this business now. I've been in it for twenty-five years. What can they teach me?," Jim probably wouldn't be able to keep my car in good running order.

Many people from various walks of life see the value of keeping their knowledge and skills current, yet teachers as a group seem to be reluctant to attend workshops and seminars. Perhaps the changes in what we know about learning don't seem as dramatic to them as breakthroughs in the medical profession or the auto industry do. And administrators too often discourage teachers from taking time away from their students to go to conferences. To attend conferences, teachers typically have to use their own sick days, pay their own way, and even pay for their own substitutes. It is little wonder that teachers give up trying to improve when their superiors make it so difficult for them.

YOU HAD TO BE THERE

In my first twelve years of teaching, I didn't attend a single conference for English teaching, though I went to several football and baseball clinics. Then, in 1978, I went with my friend Frank Gallo to Albany for a two-day state conference. I was hooked! For the first time, I felt the excitement and energy of being with like-minded teachers who had been working hard day after day, yet who had come to learn and to celebrate teaching English. The four-hour car ride there and back, the discussions over dinner and in the hotel room at night, the conversations with other teachers in between sessions were all new and enjoyable to me. Suddenly I was involved in deep discussions about issues connected to teaching, instead of in trivial chitchat exchanged while waiting for the copy machine. My teaching began to change as my horizons broadened. I began reading professional books and immersed myself in the theories underlining teaching and learning.

After several years of state conferences, I saw signs proclaiming "The English are coming!" The National Council of Teachers of English (NCTE) convention would be held in Boston in the fall. Since Boston was relatively near, some fellow English teachers and I decided to make the journey, leaving on a Saturday morning and returning home on the Wednesday evening just before Thanksgiving. The experience was like going from the minor leagues to the majors, from off-Broadway to Broadway: The state conferences were excellent, but the national conference was this and much more. The number of available workshops went from a handful each hour to thirty or more, and they went on for several days. I could have my fill of workshops covering a wide range of topics.

I became such an advocate of professional conferences that I once suggested to a principal that I take several teachers with me to conferences. He explained that the policy in the district was to allow the department chairperson to attend these conferences and then pass along the information to the rest of the teachers in the department. I replied, "So, that means I can send my English 11 class to the cafeteria, and just keep one kid who'll then explain to the rest of the class what he learned." The principal responded, "Are you suggesting that our teachers are like our students?" And I said, "Exactly! We're talking about learning and the need to be present with the expert, not accept someone else's rendition. That's the very nature of learning together, having the experience of reacting and interacting with the subject matter." I added that not letting teachers attend conferences is like not allowing fans to attend a concert or a sports contest, then asking somebody who was present to try to explain it to those who weren't. You just had to be there.

A GIFT TO ONESELF

One year, a friend who had been a regular attendee at the NCTE conference received a present from her mother, a check to help pay a substantial part of the costs of attending the convention, with a promise of a similar gift every year. Now Linda would no longer need to worry each year about how she'd be able to attend. The idea of a gift struck me. I realized that I had been giving a gift to myself, scraping together money each year to treat myself to this enriching, energizing retreat. When others asked why I attended conferences, even when the district paid no more than 10 percent of the cost, I repeated that I was "giving a gift to myself each year—something I love and something I deserve." Some teachers complain that people who work in business are sent to conferences, all expenses paid, without question. But we teachers are not in business. I won't deny myself this means of upgrading my skills and my knowledge, even though schools don't see the value of conferences. I return home each time fortified and eager to get back to my job.

After my first NCTE conference, I returned the following year, this time to Washington, D.C. The next year it was Denver. And by now, others from our district were coming to the conference for the first time. We began to pass information to first-time attendees about selecting good workshops, leaving early when a presentation was not what was expected, spending money so that it would last, and other ways to get the most out of the conference. As wise conference-goers, we realized that to make sure we'd be able to attend next year's conference, we had to come to the present one, then figure out how to convince those back home that our attendance was beneficial.

Most important, we remembered the students we had left with substitutes and their perceptions of what a conference for teachers actually was. Since many publishers began sponsoring book signings by young adult authors, I waited in lines to buy books for my classes at a dollar a book. Often, I would preview the convention program to see who the authors would be, and I'd offer to purchase a book for my students by an author of their choice, sometimes even signed by that author. Occasionally, I would buy a book for a special student and have the author write a personal inscription. Always, I would return with books to give away in class, asking students to read them and give me their opinions so I could order copies for the following year. I was paving the way for going to the next conference by creating a positive perception in my students. If my students talked about school at home, I hoped that they would report that their English teacher had returned from a conference with books for the class—perhaps even with a book for that particular student.

I also wanted to create a positive impression of the conference in the minds of my supervisors, so I would bring them promotional gifts from the exhibit hall. I would return with canvas bags, pens, note pads, and other items. I brought something back for each teacher in the English department, including sample textbooks and other materials that they could use for their classes. At department meetings, faculty members who had gone to conferences would always make brief presentations to the rest of the teachers. I would send a memo announcing my report to my supervisors, making sure that they realized the benefits of my attending the conference. I always sent a personalized thank-you note to those same people, thanking them for allowing me to continue to update my skills and knowledge.

FAST APPLICATION

When Jerry and I returned from a conference trip, we would "TRIP"—put Theory and Research Into Practice. We would ask each other what idea or activity we would use with our students upon our return. We learned from experience how easy it was to return from a workshop with an armload of good materials only to have them sit on a shelf untried because of a delay in implementation. We knew that if we tried something right away, we were more likely to get the benefit from it. Then we would tell each other about the lesson and begin to exchange materials and approaches. I always told my students when the day's lesson was a result of a conference I had attended and asked for their response to it. I continued to create positive student perceptions of my being absent from class so I could improve my teaching.

THE VALUE OF PROFESSIONAL ORGANIZATIONS

In addition to attending conferences, teachers derive nourishment and support from belonging to professional teacher organizations. In my beginning years of attending state and national conferences, I took for granted the time, planning, and hard work that went into putting on these conventions. In time, I began to meet the people who work to ensure successful experiences for conference attendees. I came to realize that these professional organizations dealt with political issues that I could not face on my own. Teachers are constantly faced with issues of censorship, class size, national standards, and standardized high-stakes testing. Special-interest groups push for positions that aren't always in the best interests of children, and teachers don't have the knowledge or the force to stand up to the pressures without professional organizations. I learned that the National Council of Teachers of English (NCTE), the New York State English Council (NYSEC), and the Long Island Language Arts Council (LILAC) act as a professional voice for me, just as other organizations do for teachers in other areas. I began to read the publications from these organizations and to develop a more informed view about the issues of the day. With today's technology, these organizations offer places for teachers to seek immediate information and support. English teachers can go to the Internet to get suggestions for a lesson, materials for a unit, advice about a problem, and support from a caring community that's ready to help at the click of a mouse. Online discussion groups, such as the subscription email lists provided by NCTE and the Conference on English Leadership (CEL), are another form of organizational support.

When I first started attending conferences, I was very impressed by the high quality of most of the presenters, never dreaming that someday I too might present a workshop. The more workshops I attended and the more books and journals I read, the more comfortable I began to feel with the material. I recognized that it was important to share some of my approaches, to pass along ideas that had been passed to me by others. And so I began to give workshops on a small scale. By taking this step, I began to find validation for what I did in the classroom when others showed appreciation for my sharing. This kind of nurturing begins with an outward gesture, seeking to teach and to encourage other teachers. It ends up with a sense of satisfaction of having helped others, a sense of satisfaction that fed my soul.

CONFERENCE TAPES

When I supervise student teachers and mention their professional organizations and the importance of their attending conferences, I follow up with a list of speakers whose talks at conferences in prior years I have on tape. Since the student teachers weren't able to attend those conferences, I help to bring the conferences to them. I ask them to listen to one of the speakers and to write a literary letter to me about what they hear. We have a lively exchange of ideas, and I conclude by suggesting other speakers they might be interested in. I let them know that I have received many benefits and great pleasure from listening to these tapes again and again. I find myself back in the conference session once more, filled with enthusiasm and delight at being there, able and willing to dine voraciously on the nourishment set forth.

11 | FINAL THOUGHTS

Please don't be misled by the subtitle of this book. "Best practices" refers to what the best practices were for me at the time. I know that not everyone will use the approaches I chose. I fear orthodoxy and worry that anyone would create "the rules" for using the principles and activities that I've related in this book. These ideas were discoveries for me as I experimented with power and control in my classroom, trying to figure things out. The impetus came from what I was learning by reading and listening to others at conferences. The implementation came from discussions with my students about how we could try out some of these ideas.

I was never without worry that I was giving students too much voice in the classroom. I debated frequently with myself or with Jerry about whether we were doing too little or too much direct teaching. I worried that I was neglecting some of the classics as I let my students select most of their own texts. Even today, I wonder if I intervened enough with reading strategies as students progressed through their varied levels of books. Are students able to take on the challenging texts of demanding college reading lists as a result of the workshop experience? I'm not always sure.

For me, it was a tradeoff. I saw how enthusiastic and productive students became when they were empowered and I remembered how limiting my classroom was when I controlled everything. Yet, like a concerned parent, I was always torn between holding on and letting go. I wanted to teach my students everything they would need for future success, but I also wanted them to become independent. It was a struggle to figure out when and how students were ready for the freedom they craved. To this day, I am still concerned that I didn't do enough with the limited days I got to share with students. When should I have talked and when should I have shut up?

In preparing this manuscript, I sent letters and emails to over fifty students seeking permission to use their writing in the book. As the document began to take shape, I found that I could not fit in more than half of the entries I had originally included. Cutting out was excruciating, so I called on my editor, Jim Strickland, to help me decide which pieces exemplified the points I was making. Nevertheless, I felt heartsick when the cuts came.

In the permission letter that I sent to former students, I asked them to think about their experience with the workshop and portfolios and to indicate ways that the experience might have helped them in their college courses and professional lives. Almost all who wrote spoke glowingly of their writing and reading experiences. Maura Brennan, a fine student who also excelled in college, said that she didn't remember writing the poem I wanted to use but what she did remember most about the workshop was "having fun that year." She went on to talk about college:

> I definitely believe that the path we followed in the reading/writing workshop was beneficial in the college classroom. One of the goals of a Jesuit education is to develop effective written and oral communication skills, and at Loyola, the freshman composition class is appropriately called "Effective Writing." The emphasis of the course is not writing a term paper, but rather the Personal Experience Narrative that I had become so familiar with in high school. Many of my classmates seemed to struggle with putting their thoughts onto paper outside of the confines of the traditional English paper. I had already learned to take risks and not to be afraid of the written word: I knew writing was fun.

Letters and emails poured in from all parts of the country. Some former students interrupted their advanced studies at medical and law schools to write to me. Some were journalists who took time from columns they were writing for magazines and newspapers. Some were still in college. Others were beginning English teachers. I heard from struggling students as well, ones who had learning deficiencies or interests outside of the academic realm. But all who replied to me celebrated their liberation to read widely, and to follow their interests and obsessions in books and in their own writing. Alan Lemley valued the demands of writing literary letters and of his class being required to read a classic together, as well as having to read some literary criticism each marking period. When it came to writing his thesis at Dartmouth, he found himself very much at home with thinking through his own ideas and articulating them in clear writing. Other replies were similar in their enthusiasm. I was stunned at the number of former students who wrote as professionals. An equal number mentioned their secret plan to write and be published, though they didn't currently work as writers.

I was thrilled to hear from these students and to read about their endeavors, as well as about their positive memories of the workshop. I know that I wasn't the only one who had helped shape these memories. Most of these readers and writers had supportive, literate parents. They had many fine teachers throughout their schooling in Miller Place. Many had actually experienced the workshop approach with other teachers in the middle school or in high school. All spoke about the skilled and dedicated teachers in the English department at Miller Place High School. The "best practices" that I used were effective because of the literate environment that surrounded these students. These conditions included schoolwide poetry readings, a packed literary magazine featuring the work of many student writers, a lively student newspaper, shared lessons and teacher collaborations, participation in writing contests, and encouragement for students to publish their work.

As I look back now upon completing this book, I marvel at how lucky I have been to have made the gigantic paradigm shift from a teacher-directed classroom to a student-centered one. I was able to learn from and with my students. The joys that I experienced in my beginning years of teaching were replaced by the joys of helping adolescents come to terms with their world by showing them how to use the power of reading and writing. All of this has softened me, made me an easy weeper, made me cherish every single moment I was entrusted by parents with their most sacred possessions, their children, my students.

My hero, the late Robert Cormier, had the courage to put his own phone number in the novel *I Am the Cheese* and then to field hundreds of phone calls over the years from respectful teenagers who wanted to ask him a question or just talk with him. In that same spirit, I include my email address for any readers who would like to ask me a question or just talk. I encourage you not to be shy and to write on! And write to me at Campyhits@aol.com.

REFERENCES

Andrasick, Kathleen Dudden. 1990. *Opening Texts: Using Writing to Teach Literature*. Portsmouth, NH: Heinemann.

Atwell, Nancie. 1987. *In the Middle: Writing, Reading, and Learning with Adolescents*. Portsmouth, NH: Boynton/Cook.

———. 1998. *In the Middle: Writing, Reading, and Learning with Adolescents*. 2d ed. Portsmouth, NH: Boynton/Cook.

———. 1992. Talk given at National Council of Teachers of English convention, November, in Louisville, KY.

———. 1995. Talk given at National Council of Teachers of English convention, in San Diego, CA.

Calkins, Lucy. 1986. *The Art of Teaching Writing*. Portsmouth, NH: Heinemann.

Cooney, Caroline B. 1990. *The Face on the Milk Carton*. New York: Bantam Doubleday Dell.

Daniels, Harvey. 1994. *Literature Circles: Voice and Choice in the Student-Centered Classroom*. York, ME: Stenhouse.

Dias, Patrick X. 1987. *Making Sense of Poetry: Patterns in the Process*. Canada: The Canadian Council of Teachers of English.

Dickinson, Emily. 1989. *Final Harvest: Emily Dickinson's Poems*. Edited by Thomas Johnson. Boston, MA: Little, Brown.

Fletcher, Ralph. 1996. *A Writer's Notebook: Unlocking the Writer Within You*. New York: Avon Books.

Gallwey, Timothy W. 1979. *The Inner Game of Golf*. New York: Random House.

Kohn, Alfie. 1993. *Punished by Rewards: The Trouble with Gold Stars, Incentive Plans, A's, Praise, and Other Bribes*. Boston: Houghton Mifflin.

———. 2000. *The Case Against Standardized Testing: Raising the Scores, Ruining the Schools*. Portsmouth, NH: Heinemann.

Kozol, Jonathan. 1998. Talk given at National Council of Teachers of English convention, November, in Nashville, TN.

Murray, Donald M. 1992. Talk given at National Council of Teachers of English convention, November, in Louisville, KY.

Noden, Harry. 1999. *Image Grammar: Using Grammatical Structures to Teach Writing.* Portsmouth, NH: Heinemann.

Ohanian, Susan. 1999. *One Size Fits Few: The Folly of Educational Standards.* Portsmouth, NH: Heinemann.

Pirie, Bruce. 2000. "Untold Stories: Culture As Activity." *The English Record* 50 (3): 12–19.

Romano, Tom. 1995. *Writing with Passion.* Portsmouth, NH: Heinemann.

Scholes, Robert. 1985. *Textual Power.* New Haven, CT: Yale University Press.

———. 1999. Talk given at National Council of Teachers of English convention, November, in Denver, CO.

INDEX

175